Speech 101

Second Custom Edition

Prof. James Como, Editor
York College, City University of New York

Excerpts taken from:

A Handbook of Public Speaking
by Richard Letteri

The Elements of Reasoning
by Edward P.J. Corbett

The Little, Brown Essential Handbook, Fifth Edition
by Jane E. Aaron

Custom Publishing

New York   Boston   San Francisco
London   Toronto   Sydney   Tokyo   Singapore   Madrid
Mexico City   Munich   Paris   Cape Town   Hong Kong   Montreal

Cover Art: *Tree in a Field*, by David Pullman.

Excerpts taken from:

A Handbook of Public Speaking, Seventh Edition
by Richard Letteri
Copyright © 2002 by Allyn & Bacon
A Pearson Education Company
Boston, Massachusetts 02116

The Elements of Reasoning
by Edward P.J. Corbett
Copyright © 1991 by Macmillan Publishing
Now published by Longman
New York, New York 10036

The Little, Brown Essential Handbook, Fifth Edition
by Jane E. Aaron
Copyright © 2005 by Pearson Education
Published by Longman

Printed in the United States of America

6 7 8 9 10   V0CR   14 13 12 11

2008560153

MT/LD

**Pearson
Custom Publishing**
is a division of

www.pearsonhighered.com

ISBN 10: 0-558-16232-0
ISBN 13: 978-0-558-16232-0

Copyright Acknowledgments

Contents

1

Research

1.1 Critical Thinking and Listening

To become a better speaker, you will need to become a critical thinker and listener. Critical listening goes beyond merely hearing the words someone speaks. It entails making a conscious effort to comprehend and evaluate the meaning of the speaker's message. Learning to analyze a **text** (e.g., a speech, written source, Internet site, interviewee, etc.) critically will allow you to gain a greater understanding of a subject and its manner of presentation. Critical thinking and listening include evaluating the information, reasoning, and appeals a source or speaker bases a claim on. Critical thinking and listening also mean paying close attention to how the text is organized and the language it uses. Along with helping you assess a text's strengths and weaknesses, such skills will help you discover your own attitudes, opinions, and presuppositions about the text's subject. In this way, you will become more aware of the limits of your own thinking and be able to view the subject more objectively. By learning how to examine other speakers and writers critically, you can learn how to become a better speaker yourself.

The following guidelines outline techniques for developing your critical thinking and listening skills. As a general rule, these techniques will help you not only to judge other speeches but also to assess critically your own speeches as well as the evidence and arguments you find in research sources.

1   Concentrate on the message.

Focus your attention on what is said and how it is said. Do not let things happening around the room distract you. Shut out any noises and other external distractions. Also, keep yourself from daydreaming and thinking about things not directly related to what the speaker is discussing.

2   Maintain a positive attitude and set aside any presuppositions you have about the speech's subject.

Do not stop listening to a speaker just because he or she is talking about something that may not interest you, is saying something that you disagree with, or is not a good speaker. Listening carefully to the speaker will open you to new ideas, new information, and new perspectives on the speaker's subject. At the very least, listening carefully will make you aware of what to avoid doing when giving your speech.

Likewise, do not let your presuppositions or prejudices deter you from listening. Instead, allow the speech to challenge your previous beliefs and understanding of the subject. Filtering a speech through your prior beliefs may cause you to put words in the speaker's mouth. You then may alter what the speaker has actually said to fit your previous understanding or attitude about the subject and thus misinterpret the speaker's point. The main point is to pay close attention to what the speaker is actually saying rather than what you *believe* he or she is or should be saying.

3   Evaluate the evidence and main parts of the speech.

Listen for the thesis statement and the main points of the speech, and determine whether the evidence provided by the speaker supports his or her thesis in a satisfactory way. Decide whether the evidence is meant to explore an idea, express an opinion, or prove a claim. Assess whether the evidence is relevant to the point or claim made, whether it is the most recent evidence and thus most applicable, and whether there is a sufficient amount of evidence presented relative to the significance of the point. Then assess the quality of the evidence: Determine whether explanations and descriptions are clear, whether the examples and statistics are strong, and whether the narratives and testimony are compelling. Also, ask yourself if other evidence would help the speaker support a point. Conversely, determine whether the arguments made are logical or fallacious. Assess whether the evidence or arguments are consistent or contradictory, whether each point coheres with the others, and whether the speaker's logical and emotional appeals are reasonable and effective. When judging the merits of an argument, consider what values or principles the claims are based on, and whether the claims are overdrawn, unreasonable, or impractical.

You also should determine whether the speech's main points are arranged in a clear and logical manner, whether each point is developed thoroughly, and whether the introduction and conclusion use the appropriate appeals. Finally, consider whether the sources cited are credible; they should hold no presuppositions, and neither the source nor the speaker should manipulate the evidence to his or her advantage.

4   Listen closely to the language and the delivery of the speech.

Ask yourself if the speaker uses the appropriate language style and delivers the speech in the best manner possible. Consider, for instance, whether the words used are too technical or if the sentences are long and difficult to follow. Similarly, study the speaker's delivery to see whether his or her changes in tone, speed, and volume and use of pauses increase the audience's understanding of the speech's points, or note how an overly monotone delivery limits the audience's understanding. Also, pay attention to gestures and movements the speaker uses, and determine how effective these nonverbal cues are and where additional gestures and movements would help the speaker relay his or her points in a more convincing manner.

As you are assessing what impact the speaker is having on you, watch how the rest of the audience responds to the speaker's language and delivery. If the speaker's wording and delivery are eliciting a positive response, consider which techniques you can incorporate into your own speaking style and delivery. If the wording and delivery are ineffective, ask yourself how you would perform the speech differently to elicit a better response.

5   Assess the overall qualities of the speech.

Although the main intent of each type of speech (informative, persuasive, ceremonial) differs, see whether the speaker strikes the appropriate balance among informing, persuading, and entertaining the audience. Evaluate the speaker's ability to explain and describe his or her subject, the analytical clarity of the evidence and arguments presented, and the way in which his or her style and delivery contribute to the overall rhetorical eloquence of the speech.

6   Compare and contrast the speech's main ideas to your own and those of other audience members.

Compare the evidence and arguments presented to those you have already heard on this or a related topic. See whether the speech adds to what you already know about the topic, changes your feelings about it, or makes you reconsider any presuppositions, prejudices, or misunderstandings you have about the topic.

Another way to compare your understanding of a subject to the way a speaker interprets it is to try to predict what the speaker will say next. Although you should not hold steadfastly to your previous beliefs, determine whether your logic is consistent with the speaker's. If it is not, assess why the speaker moved in another direction, what his or her choice adds or subtracts from your understanding of the subject, and what his or her decision says about how you and the speaker view the subject differently.

You should also listen carefully to the comments made by other audience members. Their responses may suggest alternative ways to explore the subject and strengthen the speaker's claims. Their positive and negative reactions may also tell you a great deal about how an audience will view the evidence, appeals, and language you plan to use in one of your speeches.

7   Consider taking notes on the speech.

If necessary, take notes to remind you of the speech's overall structure and its main ideas. Try to write down a brief phrase that indicates each main element or point in the speech's introduction, body, and conclusion. You might want to use various abbreviations, such as "personal" for a personal narrative, "two-sided" for a two-sided argument, and "norm" for a normative appeal, to record what type of evidence or appeals the speaker uses. You should also indicate whether you agree ("yes") or disagree ("no") with a point and try to paraphrase statements you do not understand or agree with so that you can ask the speaker about them if there is time for questions afterwards.

1.2 Selecting Your Topic

Although you can create a speech on just about any subject, selecting a good speech topic takes considerable thought and effort. Good speech topics address issues that are not only important and timely, but also are relevant and interesting to your audience. They shed new light on an old subject, address an idea from a different perspective, or take a position on a controversy. In addition, the amount of research material you find on your topic, your ability to create a strong thesis statement, and your development of interesting themes throughout the speech all play a role in turning a good speech topic into a good speech. The following guidelines offer an effective strategy for developing a list of possible topics, choosing one that best fits your speech assignment, and refining your topic's focus so that your audience will find it significant and interesting.

1   Begin by brainstorming.

Develop potential speech topics by listing as many ideas as possible. At first, do not criticize any ideas. Simply write down whatever comes to mind, no matter how general or specific the subject is. Begin by brainstorming on topics that interest you and that you would like to learn more about.

When brainstorming, start with subjects that readily come to mind because they are of personal interest to you. Consider topics that relate to a class you took recently, a trip you plan to take, or a job or internship you hope to obtain. Likewise, list topics that relate to subjects that you always wanted to learn about but were never given the opportunity to study, or a current event that you have been following in the news. Also, write down topics that involve volunteer work you do or a personal hobby you enjoy such as working at an animal shelter or swing dancing.

After exhausting these topics, turn next to more traditional speech topics such as important persons, places, and events. Write down the names of significant individuals in history, politics, or religion. Also, consider doing a speech on your favorite author or artist. Similarly, list the names of major cities, exciting community festivals, or noteworthy monuments or geographical areas you have visited or would like to know more about. You should also consider doing a speech on how some recent scientific research, technological innovation, or archeological discovery has dramatically changed how we will live in the future or understand the past.

You can also develop topics that deal with more practical, everyday concerns such as a new computer software product, a profitable investment strategy, a popular diet plan, or an innovative exercise routine. How to repair a mountain bike, where to take an inexpensive vacation, and what nutritional value various types of ethnic foods have are also speech topics that your audience may find interesting and relevant.

If you are interested in political and social issues, think about topics that concern anything from welfare and educational policy, to health care and environmental concerns, to media violence and teen pregnancy. These speech topics can cover areas as large as international trade, a peace treaty between nations, a worldwide epidemic, and global warming; or areas as small as local city zoning, a truce between neighborhood street gangs, ways to prevent spreading the flu, or your university's recycling program.

Finally, consider topics that are unusual, such as why a manual laborer gave a large amount of money to a charity, or how a famous work of art was discovered to be a forgery. You can also list topics that are sensational or controversial. Such topics can include a well-publicized legal case, a natural disaster, a strange religious belief, or a hotly debated Hollywood movie. Similarly, consider doing a speech on such paranormal phenomena as extrasensory perception or UFOs.

2   **To discover more topics, check reference indexes, browse the Internet, and skim through some major newspapers, periodicals, and academic journals.**

Peruse your library's reference system, databases, and the Internet for potential topics. Skim through printed sources for articles that discuss important issues that you can rework into a speech topic. The research sources listed in this chapter cover a variety of potential subjects for speeches that may interest both you and your audience.

3   **Generate new topics from those you have already listed.**

Start by narrowing topics that are overly broad so that you can thoroughly explore your subject in the time allotted to you. For example, you can limit a speech on campus life to the difficulties foreign exchange students face in a new academic environment. Likewise, rework a speech on health maintenance organizations (HMOs) to one that deals specifically with how many HMO health policies do not pay for mental health care. Also consider reworking older topics into newer ones. For instance, instead of doing a speech on the Italian mafia, focus on the Russian mafia or Colombian drug cartels.

Next, think about how you can turn a topic that is overly general or personal to one that is more unique and significant. Instead of giving a speech on why you are a football fanatic, consider doing a speech on English soccer hooligans. Also think about how you can relate a current event to a matter of continual interest and importance. For example, turn a speech on racism into one about how hate groups are using the Internet to recruit members. Or provide a context for a great piece of literature by discussing those historical events that shaped the author's portrayal of the events and characters in the book.

Finally, consider addressing issues or characteristics of a familiar topic that are not often discussed. In this case, instead of describing the damage caused by a hurricane, debate whether local governments should fix the prices of goods and services after a natural disaster. In addition, try developing alternative ways to interpret a topic. For instance, instead of explaining the political events surrounding a terrorist act, offer a psychological portrait of a terrorist.

4 After accumulating enough topics, select those that will be the most significant and appealing to your audience.

Choose subjects that your audience will find interesting, informative, and entertaining. Just as you ask questions that help you determine which topics interest you, ask whether your audience would find a topic appealing because it affects them personally, because it offers a solution to a significant problem, or because it deals with a controversial topic. In addition, you can engage an audience by discussing new information about a topic. For example, in light of recent DNA studies, your audience may be interested in a speech on Thomas Jefferson's relationship with Sally Hemming. You can also try addressing a common topic from a new perspective. Thus, rather than giving a speech on baseball, give one on why children should not throw certain types of pitches that may injure their underdeveloped arm muscles.

When considering your audience, however, do not underestimate their willingness to listen to a speech about a topic audience members initially view as difficult or unappealing. By discovering interesting evidence and making the appropriate appeals, you can engage even a reluctant audience.

5 Identify those topics that best fit your speech assignments.

After determining which of your topics are the most interesting, consider which topic best fits the type of speech you are assigned to give. For an informative speech, look for a topic you can clearly define, classify, or describe. If you are assigned a demonstrative speech, choose a topic that lets you perform an activity relating to it. The best demonstrative topics are those you can break down into clear, distinct steps that your audience can follow easily. When preparing a persuasive speech, choose a topic that entails some controversy or issue on which you can take a position and construct arguments that support your position. For a policy speech, your topic must concern how an organization has failed to deal adequately with a problem or to provide services to its constituents, and your plan to improve the situation.

6 Consider ways to modify a topic to fit the requirements of your speaking situation.

The main components of your speaking situation are the time allotted for your speech, its setting, the mode of your delivery, and your audience's attitude toward your topic. Because people's attitudes are often shaped by such things as their age, sex, race, income, values, beliefs, personal interests, and what sources they usually obtain their information from, consider how these factors may influence your audience's reception of your speech.

7   **Determine whether you have the appropriate facilities, knowledge, and time to research your topic.**

Consider whether you can obtain important information and other material relating to your topic. Ask yourself such questions as

- Does my library have the sources I need?
- Do I have the material that I need for my demonstrative speech?
- Can I obtain media and computer aids for my presentation?
- Who are the individuals I would like to interview for my speech?

Also, although you will learn more about your topic through your research, consider whether you have enough prior knowledge of the topic to understand the evidence and arguments you will find. Ask yourself,

- Do I understand the main terms relating to my topic?
- Will I be able to explain clearly the evidence I find?
- Do I know enough about my topic that I can weigh arguments for or against it?

Last, plan how much time you will need to research, organize, and practice your speech. Consider making a schedule that designates how much time you will need to do library research, conduct interviews, and gather additional materials for your speech. Then determine how much time you will need to complete your outline or manuscript and how long it will take to practice delivering your speech. You must also set aside some time to evaluate your speech critically. When evaluating your speech, ask yourself questions such as

- Are there better ways to introduce or conclude my speech?
- Do any of my main points lack strong supportive evidence?
- Do the various parts of my speech fit together into a unified whole?
- Have I chosen the best words, phrases, and sentence structures for expressing my point?

If you answer "no" to any of these questions, you will need to take the time to do some additional research or rewrite your speech.

1.3 Researching Your Topic

Once you have a general idea of what your topic will be, you are ready to begin your research. Although some topics may require you to pursue your research differently, one of the best ways to discover information on your topic is first to look for general background material on your topic and then pursue more recent and specific sources. The research strategy given here follows this basic process.

1   Develop a list of key terms that will help you gather information on your topic.

Create a preliminary list of important issues, ideas, facts, people, and dates that you will want to discuss in your speech. One way to develop this list is to employ the journalistic technique of asking questions about the who, what, where, when, why, and how of your topic. For example, ask such questions as the following:

- Who are the most important people relating to my topic?
- Who are the premier authorities on my topic?
- Who is affected the most by my topic?
- What is the best way to define my topic?
- What are the most important issues relating to my topic?
- What are the important facts relating to my topic?
- What are the main organizations and associations that deal with my topic?
- What are the main newspapers, periodicals, academic journals, and so on that discuss my topic?
- Where are the places that are most affected by my topic?
- When was my topic born or created, or when did it happen?
- When did people become interested in my topic?
- Why is my topic important to people?
- Why is my topic controversial?
- How has my topic changed through time?
- How does my topic relate to people's immediate concerns?
- How does my topic relate to other important issues?

Use your answers to these questions to create the key terms you will use to search the various sources described next.

2   **To gather general information on your topic, consult encyclopedias, almanacs, books, other types of reference material, as well as your librarian.**

Become better acquainted with your topic by first going to research sources that present a general overview of your subject. Both general and specialized encyclopedias are good places to find background information such as historical facts and definitions relating to your topic. An encyclopedia also can provide you with other types of helpful information. For instance, how an encyclopedia divides your topic into subject areas can suggest ways to organize the main points of your speech. Moreover, pay close attention to how an encyclopedia explains your topic. Because an encyclopedia is written for a general reading audience, the terms and writing style it uses may suggest ways to present your topic that your audience can easily understand. Also, most encyclopedias offer a brief but authoritative bibliography that may contain additional sources for your speech.

Other reference sources, such as almanacs and statistical abstracts, may provide additional information about your topic. These sources organize statistical data in a variety of ways. For instance, they can provide information on the scope of your topic, how it has changed over time, or the ways it is classified by region, gender, or race. You can find almanacs and statistical abstracts, as well as encyclopedias, in your library's reference section, on a database, and on the Internet.

Finally, after doing some preliminary research, ask a librarian to help find information on your subject. Librarians know their library's holdings better than anyone and have helped people conduct research on most every subject. Their suggestions can help you to find more information as well as to use your time in the library more efficiently.

3   **Use your library's electronic catalogue to search its holdings.**

Your library's electronic catalogue system indexes the books, news periodicals, academic journals, government documents, videotapes, and other research materials in its present collection. Use your key terms, particularly the names of the authors, titles of books, and possible subject headings to search for materials pertaining to your topic. You should also combine various key words with the search operators and techniques.

4   **Search your library's databases and the Internet for more specific and current sources dealing with your topic.**

Databases are electronic indexes that provide either references to sources or the actual sources themselves, be they articles published in newspapers, periodicals, or academic journals, transcripts from radio and television shows, or government documents. The Internet also provides access to many of these same sources as well as to a host of web sites maintained by media outlets, private individuals and associations, scholars, and government agencies. Thus, both databases and the Internet provide access to a variety of sources that discuss a vast array of subjects. Moreover, using databases and the Internet can help you find some of the most specific and up-to-date information concerning your topic.

5 Interview government officials, scholars, professionals, administrators, experts, and witnesses for their testimonies and opinions on your topic.

An interview may provide you with unpublished recent or personal information that cannot be obtained elsewhere. In addition, audiences appreciate the extra effort it takes to acquire this information. If you are going to interview someone, make sure that you complete most of your research beforehand so that you appear knowledgeable about your subject and so that you prepare an effective list of interview questions.

6 Document your information and its sources.

Use a separate note card or sheet of paper for each piece of evidence. Placing each piece of evidence on a separate note will allow you to arrange your evidence in your outline more easily.

When conducting your research, take notes on all the relevant information. You do not have to copy information verbatim. Rather, you can save time by summarizing long passages and commonly known information and by paraphrasing information that you will not quote directly. Remember, however, to avoid plagiarizing from your original sources.

To save time and ensure accuracy, you might want to photocopy those sources that contain a great deal of pertinent information. When retrieving information from a database or a web site, you may be able to transfer the information onto a computer file (or send it to your e-mail box), and then print it out. Once you have the information as it appeared originally, you can then, literally or electronically, cut and paste information onto note cards.

Another important way to document your source is to indicate whether you have summarized (S), paraphrased (P), or directly quoted from (" ") the source. In addition, consider using headings to suggest where you might use the information in your speech (e.g., "Introduction," "First main point") or what function it might serve (e.g., "Anecdote," "Evidence against the status quo").

Finally, make sure you copy all the relevant bibliographic information pertaining to the source of your information, such as the author, title, volume number, date, publisher, and page numbers.

7   Begin evaluating your evidence and organizing it into an outline.

After completing your initial search, determine what your strongest, most credible evidence is, and then begin determining what your main points and subpoints will be. Omit any evidence that is weak, overly technical, and irrelevant to the overall purpose of your speech. Nevertheless, do not select only that evidence which fits your working thesis statement. Rather, change your thesis to fit the evidence you have found.

Next, determine which organizational structure will allow you to arrange your evidence most effectively, and arrange your information accordingly.

Last, as mentioned earlier, realize that when preparing and practicing your speech, you may discover that you need additional material, such as a strong quotation or statistic, to support a point. Hence, be prepared to look for more information whenever necessary.

2

Organization

2.1 General Speech Structure

The following outline provides the general framework for organizing most informative or persuasive speeches. [Ceremonial speeches often follow different organizational guidelines.] This general structure should be understood as a basic model that you can adopt completely or modify to satisfy the needs of your particular speech. Consider how you can combine, omit, or alter elements of the general speech structure to present your particular topic, thesis statement, evidence, and appeals in the most effective manner possible. For instance, by beginning your speech with a personal narrative, you can simultaneously perform the first two functions of an introduction. You also can combine the audience response step in your conclusion with your closing remarks.

1   Introduction

Gain and maintain your audience's attention.   The function of your opening statement is to stimulate your audience's interest in your topic. There are many different techniques for sparking your audience's interest. You can begin by describing an important historical or current event affected by your topic or by defining a particular aspect of your topic that you will return to later in your speech. You also can clarify a popular misunderstanding about your topic or illustrate it with an insightful statistic, fact, or authoritative statement. If you want to take a more indirect approach, begin with a series of questions alluding to your topic, or employ a pun on your speech's title or subject matter. However, never begin by apologizing for being unprepared, ridiculing your topic, telling your audience you are nervous, or denouncing your speaking abilities. Trying to decrease you audience's expectations may cause you to lose credibility.

Relate your topic to your audience.   After sparking your audience's interest in your topic, show its significance. By establishing your topic's significance early in your speech, you supply your audience with good reasons to listen attentively to the whole speech. One of the best ways to characterize your topic's importance is to relate it to your audience's immediate or future concerns. For example, you can describe how your topic affects society or how it influences the way your audience thinks and acts. You also can state how your speech will add to your audience's general understanding of your topic.

Relate your topic and audience to yourself.   It is often important to begin building your *ethos,* or credibility as a speaker, in your introduction. There are three main ways to build your credibility. You can verify your knowledge of your topic by referring to personal experiences or training you have with respect to your topic, or by describing your research and citing your main research sources. You can also build your credibility by tying your views on your topic to a value that your audience holds. Establishing an ethical basis for how you will treat your topic will help you gain your audience's trust and support. Last, consider expressing empathy with your audience's perception of and concerns about your topic so that they will see you as someone who understands their needs and interests and can help fulfill them.

State your thesis, and forecast the organization of your speech.   After stimulating your audience's interest and relating yourself and your topic to your audience, explain the intent of your speech and outline its general structure. That is, state your thesis and give a brief summary of your main points. Together, your thesis and preview summary should clarify your speech's purpose, preview its overall structure, and show how each main point will explicate your thesis statement. Moreover, consider using your thesis statement and preview summary to reinforce your topic's significance or the mutual values you and your audience hold with respect to your topic.

2   Body

Divide your topic into your main points.   Your main points consist of the central ideas, issues, processes, arguments, and so on, that you will explore in your speech. All of your main points must provide information that will fulfill the intent of your thesis statement. Your speech should consist of three to five main points that you want to elucidate or prove. Each main point should be a distinct idea that can stand on its own. At the same time, each main point should relate clearly to your thesis and to every other main point. Your main points should have relatively the same degree of significance and the same number of subpoints, and should be allotted approximately the same amount of time within your speech. When organizing your main points, consider adopting one (or a combination) of the organizational patterns or types of speeches that best suits your topic, thesis statement, and main points.

Provide evidence for your main points.   A **subpoint** is a piece of evidence that supports your main points. Similarly, a **sub-subpoint** provides evidence in support of a subpoint. In general, use explanations, descriptions, statistics, examples, analogies, narratives, and testimonies, as well as the other types of evidence and arguments, to explain, define, or prove each of your main points and subpoints.

Use transitions to unify your speech.   Transitions are statements or phrases that relate the various parts of your speech to one another and thus help to unify your speech. There are many different types of transitions, each of which performs a distinct function. The three main types of transitions are preview transitions, which foreshadow what is to come in your speech; review transitions, which summarize what you have already said; and signpost transitions, which enumerate various points in your speech.

3   Conclusion

Forewarn your audience that you are about to conclude.   Indicate that you are going to conclude by saying something such as "In conclusion," or simply suggest that you are concluding by using a long pause and then raising your tone. Along with signaling that you are concluding, you may want to begin developing your concluding statement at this point by returning to a theme or motif used earlier in your speech or introducing a new theme that embodies the functions and sentiment of your conclusion.

Review the main parts of your speech.   Review your speech by summarizing your thesis statement and main points. When summarizing, do not refer vaguely to the general content of your speech. Rather, succinctly reexplain how your main points and subpoints provided evidence for your thesis statement. To provoke your audience's memory, you may want to restate specifically your most important pieces of evidence. Alternatively, try summarizing your speech by providing new evidence that is consistent with the evidence you already have given in your speech. When used appropriately, this technique will allow your audience to see your subject from a new perspective while simultaneously reminding them of your main points.

Strengthen your audience's positive response to your speech.   Highlight the shared ethical grounds you have established between you, your topic, and your audience to build on the ethical and emotional bond you have established with them in order to ensure their favorable response to your speech. You also can explain how your speech allows your audience to understand your topic more completely or differently than before, or suggest ways they can explore your topic further or interpret another, similar subject in light of the information you have provided.

End your speech.   End your speech with a concluding statement that brings closure to your speech and captures your speech's purpose. Some of the main ways to conclude a speech are to offer a quotation that captures your thesis, ask a rhetorical question that highlights the problem you have addressed, employ a figure of speech that captures your convictions, or give an optimistic statement about the future. Regardless of the technique you choose, do not end your speech by stating, apathetically, that you are finished speaking. Rather, offer a concluding statement that captures at least one of the main ideas, aims, or sentiments of your speech.

2.2 Introductory and Concluding Statements

How you begin and end your speech can greatly influence the way your audience receives your speech and how they will remember it. Thus, your speech's introduction and conclusion are as important as its body. Because your introduction and conclusion are so integral to your speech, they should be consistent with the general tone and content of the main points in your speech's body. Together, all three parts of your speech should create a unified whole.

One way to unify your speech is to seek **closure** by weaving the evidence or appeals from your introduction into your speech's body and conclusion. By referring back to a piece of evidence, an appeal, or a motif used earlier in your speech, the technique of closure not only unifies your speech, but also gives the evidence or appeal greater meaning and significance at your speech's end. Although the examples presented in this section all show how to achieve closure, you do not always have to use the same type of statement to begin and end your speech. Rather, you can use any of these types of statements as long as each fulfills the main purpose of an introductory or concluding statement.

The main functions of your introductory statement are to gain your audience's attention and to make them more receptive to your speech and thesis. The main functions of your concluding statement are to capture the purpose of your speech and to evoke those sentiments you want your audience to feel as a result of your speech. In many instances, you will want to end your speech with an optimistic statement about the future. Thus, your concluding statement could stress how your speech provides your audience with a better understanding of your subject or how your proposed solution will make their lives better. However, you do not always have to end on an optimistic note; rather, leave your audience with a sense of how they should view your subject regardless of whether it is a feeling of optimism or pessimism, harmony or conflict, hope or despair.

When constructing your introductory or concluding statements, consider using one of these techniques, many of which are types of evidence that have been explained in more depth earlier.

1   Shock.

Use a startling statement, story, or other piece of evidence to spark your audience's interest and stir their emotions. This technique is best used when you are facing an inattentive or reluctant audience, when you want to create a confrontational atmosphere, or when your topic, on its surface, appears unoriginal or uninteresting. As a concluding technique, shocking your audience may create a strong and lasting impact.

INTRODUCTION
Every one of you in this room deserves to be in jail! Why? Because unless you are doing everything possible to control government spending, you are stealing money from your children and your grandchildren!

CONCLUSION

Let me end by telling you the good news. You have all been granted a pardon. But you must promise to work together to limit uncontrolled government spending. If you do not, your children have every right to take away your social security and leave you desperate on the streets. Given the way you are allowing this government to destroy their future, don't think they won't do it!

2   Statistics.

Presenting statistics frames your subject in a clear and rational way. Thus, beginning or ending your speech with statistical evidence may add to your credibility. The two main ways to use statistics in an introductory statement are to show the scope of your subject, or to surprise, even shock, your audience with data they are unaware of.

INTRODUCTION

Most people accept alcohol consumption as a normal part of daily life. But recently, the Department of Justice announced that four out of every ten fatal car crashes in America involve alcohol. Similarly, the *Christian Science Monitor* reports that eighty to ninety percent of all crimes involve alcohol. In Maine, half of adults surveyed said that someone in their family has a serious alcohol problem. Perhaps the time has come to rethink our attitudes toward alcohol.

CONCLUSION

When you put all the facts together, alcohol consumption should be treated as a public health problem, not as a normal part of our lives. Prohibition clearly is not the answer. But when half the families in Maine have to watch their loved ones slowly destroy themselves, we must recognize that we are dealing with a public health emergency. Perhaps we can all learn from the state of Minnesota. According to a 1996 issue of the *Harvard Mental Health Letter,* the state of Minnesota found alcohol treatment reduced crime rates by sixty-six percent and alcohol use by forty percent. Such numbers show us that an effective solution is close at hand.

3   Testimony.

Whether it is from an authority or someone who has direct experience with your subject, begin and end your speech with a testimony. By quoting someone with expertise in your topic, you implicitly transfer his or her credibility to you. Testimony also can lend authenticity to your speech when you provide statements from individuals who have real-life experiences with your subject. When offering testimony, try to find quotations that offer either vivid descriptions of the person's experience, or direct and forceful declarations of the authority's position.

INTRODUCTION

"It happened fast," reports Joe McBride, president of the Montauk Boatmen and Captains Association. "We used to fish for brown or sandbar sharks in the summertime. Now, we are lucky to see one of them because they are so overfished down south." According to the December 23, 1997, issue of *Newsday*, Mr. McBride's comments are consistent with the conclusions of scientific experts, who have found an alarming decline of sharks around the world. "The best available data says we are fishing sharks twice as fast as they can reproduce," says Sonja Fordham, fisheries specialist for the Center for Marine Conservation.

CONCLUSION

In this speech I have tried to show just how threatened these beautiful and mysterious animals are. You should also know that even our best efforts to solve this problem might not be enough. As Jack Musick of the Virginia Institute of Marine Science says, "Even in the rosiest scenario, it is going to take at least a decade to make progress in restoring stocks."

4   Narrative.

Whether you use a report, anecdote, or story, a narrative can create concrete, evocative images through which your audience may experience your subject. Your narrative should be long enough that your audience recognizes it is a story, but short enough that their minds do not begin to wander.

INTRODUCTION

The story is frightening. "It was twilight in Sudan when U.S. missiles tore across the horizon and then three explosions lit up the darkening sky," recounts the *New York Daily News*. "At that instant, other American cruise missiles screaming through the Hindu Kush mountain range were striking a rugged corner of Afghanistan. The simultaneous cruise missile attacks came without warning and were so swift their targets didn't know what hit them. State-run Sudan television interrupted its programming to announce that the country was 'subjected to an aerial strike by American warplanes that aimed at strategic targets.' Sudanese television aired graphic footage of the factory in flames and rescuers wearing surgical masks over their faces as they pulled the wounded from the twisted metal. It was not clear if there were any dead."

CONCLUSION

I began this speech with a story of the ugly reality of the war against terrorism. But let's step back eleven days before those U.S. cruise missiles struck. "She already knew that her son was dead," reported the *New York Times*. "But as Sue Bartley and one-hundred fifty other mourners left a memorial service . . . for the American victims of Friday's terrorist bombing, they were hoping against hope that Mrs. Bartley's husband, Consul General Julian Bartley, was still alive. They listened to a reading from Ecclesiastes, heard a mournful taps, then went home to wait, grasping red roses in trembling hands. Within hours, their wisp of hope was gone. Using torn clothing, strands of hair and a ring, doctors positively identified Mr. Bartley's badly disfigured body this evening, adding his name to a list of eleven dead Americans that included the Bartley's twenty-year-old son, Jay." This dramatic account of Sue Bartley's pain should provide reason enough to explain why President Clinton's actions were necessary.

5   Current event.

Relating your topic to a current event helps establish your topic's significance by associating it with events that most likely are on your audience's mind. This technique also provides you with an effective way to take your audience from the outside world into your speech and back out again.

INTRODUCTION

If you have been following the news lately, you probably watched the progress of Steve Fosset as he attempted to become the first person to fly a hot air balloon around the world. Of course, Fosset did not make it. He crashed into the cold, stormy sea and was lucky to be rescued. But Fosset knew the enormous risks he faced, and still he persevered. He did not let his fear get the better of him. Fosset was not afraid to risk it all because he believed the reward is worth it. Similarly, Tom Roberts believed that building a family business was worth the effort, and so he spent his life working to achieve his dream.

CONCLUSION

Hot air ballooning is not for everybody. Some of you may even think that Steve Fosset's goal was ridiculous. But it meant a great deal to him, and that's the point. He refused to surrender to fear. He believed that he had not yet achieved his dream, and so he gave it his best. Tom, you gave it your best, and now your dream is your family's future.

6   Analogy.

Analogies allow you to put complex ideas in terms that your audience can more easily understand. Using an analogy to introduce a complicated subject may allow your audience to become more comfortable with your speech. Whether introducing or concluding your speech, use descriptive language to build your analogy.

INTRODUCTION

Ronald Reagan once compared the Soviet Union to an octopus whose powerful tentacles were poised to stretch out around the world to devour freedom-loving nations. But today, the red octopus has washed ashore and finds itself helpless and desperately seeking to survive in the new-world economy.

CONCLUSION
By all accounts, Russia is no longer the powerful octopus it was during the Soviet era. But some of you may recall walking along the beach and finding a stranded creature of some kind or another. Maybe you even poked it with a stick to see if it was still alive. If you did, you probably jumped six feet in the air when it suddenly moved. The same principle holds true for Russia. It may be sleeping, but its tentacles are still powerful.

7   Humor.

Using humor is an effective way of capturing your audience's attention and putting them at ease. A concluding remark, joke, anecdote, or pun can leave your audience with an amiable feeling. Whichever you choose, always tie your humor directly to your point, avoid telling elaborate and offensive jokes, and use humor sparingly so that you are not perceived as lacking seriousness.

INTRODUCTION
"There's no time like the present." You've all heard this familiar saying a thousand times. However, you have probably never heard the next line, which is, "Especially if it's for me!" Yes, time really is a valuable gift, but we should never be selfish about it. So today I want to urge you to spend your time productively by volunteering to help others.

CONCLUSION
They say, "big things come in small packages." I learned that well when I told my mother I wanted a Mustang for my high school graduation, and she gave me the Hotwheels version of the car. Still, the greatest gift she gave me was her time, attention, and love; and there was nothing small about that. By volunteering a little bit of your time, you can mean something big to someone who needs your help.

8   Rhetorical question.

A rhetorical question is a question whose answer is often readily apparent. Beginning your speech with a rhetorical question entices your audience into thinking about the purpose of your speech without stating it directly. Closing your speech with a rhetorical question is an effective way to keep your audience thinking about your speech's purpose long after you conclude.

INTRODUCTION
Who was more loyal to the Cleveland Browns, the owner, who moved the team to Baltimore for a better stadium deal, or the people of

Cleveland? Unfortunately, in professional sports today, both owners as well as athletes are loyal to only one thing: money. Pursuing the almighty dollar may be good for players and owners, but it hurts the team, their fans, the league, and ultimately, the game, no matter what professional sport it is.

CONCLUSION

If Michael Jordan had left the Bulls before retiring, would anyone have remembered what team he played for in his last years? Probably not. In the minds of his fans, Michael Jordan will always be a Chicago Bull. However, many of today's sport's superstars think of themselves as temp workers, and many team owners think of themselves as corporate raiders. Their lack of commitment hurts not only the teams' host cities and their fans, but also the games we all love to watch.

9   Affirming a value.

Introducing or concluding your speech with a value supported by your audience increases the likelihood that they will accept your thesis. Tying your claims to a commonly held value may also build your credibility. Affirming a value you share with a receptive audience allows you to solidify their agreement with your thesis quickly and may allow you to move them to act on it. Moreover, beginning your speech by affirming a value can effectively and quickly win over a potentially unreceptive audience. In a similar way, ending your speech by affirming a shared value may leave your audience with a lasting positive image of you and your topic.

INTRODUCTION

The Judeo-Christian tradition is clear in saying that one of our greatest moral duties is to love our neighbors as ourselves. People of all faiths and no faith alike can agree that this moral principle indeed should be "the golden rule." If we do not treat others with tolerance and respect, how can we expect anything but intolerance and disrespect from them? That is why today I want to convince you that we should affirm the rights of homosexuals to marry.

CONCLUSION

In conclusion, if you are not willing to give homosexuals the right to marry, then you are necessarily supporting a system that would allow homosexuals to deny heterosexuals the right to marry if they were in the majority. Christ was right: We should love our neighbors as ourselves. That does not mean we have to do what they do or believe what they believe, but it does mean we have to respect their values as we would want them to respect ours.

10   Stating your thesis.

In most instances, you do not want to begin or end your speech with your thesis statement. On rare occasions, however, you should consider beginning and ending your speech with your thesis statement. Some such occasions are when you want to create a sense of candor and directness, when you want to stress your position, or when the amount of evidence you want to discuss leaves little time for an introductory or concluding statement.

INTRODUCTION
The number of unplanned teenage pregnancies has reached such epidemic proportions that we must do everything we can to combat this grave social problem. Today I want to propose a policy that integrates the services of government agencies and schools with those of nongovernmental agencies, such as churches and women's groups, to solve the problem of teenage pregnancy.

CONCLUSION
Unplanned teenage pregnancies in America must be reduced. To reduce teen pregnancies, we must combine the funding, staffing, and services of government agencies with those provided by schools, churches, and women's groups. The only way we can solve the problem of teenage pregnancy is to pull together the resources of all these public and private institutions. I hope you agree and will support my plan.

2.3 Thesis Statement and Preview Summary

Your thesis statement declares the intent of your speech. It should state the main subject, purpose, and ideas you will discuss. Your preview summary shows how each of your main points will develop your thesis. Together, your thesis and preview summary establish the purpose of your speech and show how you will fulfill that purpose. The guidelines offered here suggest how to develop an effective thesis statement and preview summary.

1   When creating your thesis statement, ask yourself questions about your speech's topic and intent.

Begin by asking yourself what topic you want to discuss and why you want to discuss it. Next, ask yourself how your audience might react to your thesis. In this sense, ask yourself why your audience would find your topic significant and why your speech is worth hearing. Likewise, ask yourself whether your potential thesis will allow you to address those issues relating to your topic that your audience will find informative, persuasive, and entertaining. Also ask how you could word your thesis so that your speech appears interesting, inviting, and morally acceptable. Finally, consider the relationship between your potential thesis and your speaking situation. Ask whether your thesis is appropriate given the setting for your speech, the time allotted to you, the audience you will speak to, and the general social conditions of the moment in which you will speak.

2   Consider the rhetorical purpose of your speech.

In general, the rhetorical purpose of a speech consists of what you want to accomplish with your speech, the impression you want to give about you and your topic, and the reaction you want to receive from your audience. The main goals of a speech are to inform, persuade, or entertain your audience—or some combination of the three. If your intent is to inform, decide what general and specific ideas, issues, and information you want your audience to know and understand about your topic as a result of your speech. When seeking to persuade, consider how you want your audience to act or think differently about your topic. Also think about what type of thesis statement, evidence, arguments, and appeals will incline them to change their perception of your topic, their personal behavior, or their public actions. If your purpose is to entertain your audience or have them commemorate a person or occasion, determine what themes, appeals, and language your audience would enjoy hearing, or which of these would bring them together in celebration.

3   Determine the specific purpose of your speech.

The specific purpose of your speech identifies the exact goals you want to achieve with your speech. In many ways, your specific purpose simply restates your rhetorical purpose in terms of the particular claim you want to pursue, ideas and evidence you want to discuss, and audience response you want to achieve. Thus, it narrowly defines your intent in terms of main issues you want your audience to consider, the precise information you want them to know, the distinct arguments you want them to agree with, and the specific response or actions you want to elicit as a result of your speech.

When determining which goals you will pursue in your speech, consider what immediate or short-term results you could accomplish and what long-term and sustained results are possible. Most of time, you will want to focus on achieving direct results, such as providing your audience with a greater understanding of your topic or persuading them to pursue some immediate action. Because changing life habits and deep-seated values takes a great deal of convincing and effort, speakers rarely hope to accomplish long-term goals and drastic results through a speech. However, you can use your speech to show your audience how they can take both immediate and future steps to reach a larger goal.

4   **Create a working thesis that reflects your rhetorical purpose, your specific purpose, the areas of the topic you want to discuss, and your potential conclusion.**

To help guide your research and develop your outline, create a working thesis that captures the specific intent of your speech and previews the areas of your topic you need to address to fulfill your purpose. Be prepared to modify this tentative thesis as you continue to collect and analyze your information. After you have a sufficient grasp of your research material, begin formulating your final thesis statement.

5   **State your thesis in a simple, declarative sentence that makes clear what you will discuss and how you will discuss it.**

Your thesis should consist of a statement that specifically addresses what you will explore or prove in your speech. It should also directly reflect the relationship you want to establish with your audience. That is, it should assert the main intention of your speech. Thus, you should directly state that you intend to inform your audience about a topic, demonstrate a set of procedures, defend or refute an argument, justify a policy, or influence your audience to act or think differently. Your thesis should then specifically state the main ideas, procedures, arguments, and so on that you will discuss. By combining these two functions, your thesis statement not only will make clear precisely what your speech is about, but will also define the role you play as a speaker and the response you hope to gain from your audience.

6   **Make sure the wording of your thesis presents your speech's intent in the clearest, most effective way possible.**

Consider how the words you use will affect your audience's reception of your thesis and speech. Do not use overly technical language that may intimidate or put off your audience. Moreover, be sure your phrasing captures your main intentions and sentiments as well as appeals to your audience. For this reason, do not exaggerate the character of your proposal when you intend to offer only a modest change in a policy, and do not use vitriolic rhetoric that may offend some members of your audience.

2.4 Patterns of Organization

1 **Directly follow your thesis statement with a preview summary of the organization of your speech.**

Your thesis statement and preview summary can be combined into one sentence or can consist of several sentences. Regardless of their structure, use your thesis statement to articulate your speech's main purpose and your preview summary to indicate how each of your main points will develop your thesis. Together, your thesis and preview summary should clarify your speech's purpose and main ideas so that your audience can establish the appropriate expectations about your speech and feel satisfied once these expectations are fulfilled.

2 **Repeat or rephrase your thesis statement throughout your speech.**

Working your thesis statement into your speech in various ways will continually remind your audience of how your thesis relates to your main points. Repeating your thesis may also increase the probability that your audience will accept your thesis. Along with stating your thesis in your introduction, you may want to rephrase it when introducing a main point, use it in a transition, and restate it when summarizing your speech in your conclusion.

EXAMPLES

Although most of you have heard of Salvador Dali and surrealism, I would like to explore further the man and this artistic movement by discussing the man, the movement, and the surrealist themes and motifs found in Dali's most famous paintings.

My intent today is to inform you about the potential dangers of exercising in the extreme heat and explain how to prevent and treat heat stroke.

In this speech, I will argue that single-sex schools and classes offer women substantial educational, social, and personal benefits that cannot be gained in a traditional, coeducational setting.

After examining the limits of the voucher system, I will show that the crisis in public education can be solved only through state initiatives that provide equal funding for all public schools.

2.5 Types of Transitions

1   Qualifying transition.

To clarify the significance of a point or characterize the relationship between points, use a qualifying transition. You can also use an argument qualifier to express the strength of the logical relationship between the premises and conclusion of an argument.

EXAMPLES

Unless

Although

Based upon the condition that

Only if

However,

It is likely that

This is only true if

Consequently,

Hence,

Therefore,

Thus, it follows that,

In all probability,

2   Relational transition.

A relational transition provides a link between points having the same or a similar significance, function, or meaning. Use a relational transition to show the relationship between your main points or to show how evidence supporting one point is similar to evidence supporting another. To emphasize the congruity between each main point, consider introducing each with the same transition, such as, "Another argument against the proposal is. . . ."

EXAMPLES

In addition,

Similarly,

Likewise,

So, just like

Another example of this is

Comparatively speaking,

This is very similar to

3   Oppositional transition.

Rather than linking similar ideas, an oppositional transition relates two points having a different meaning or significance. Consider using an oppositional transition when showing different perspectives on the same point, distinguishing between opposing arguments, or discussing the strengths and weaknesses of a point.

EXAMPLES

This is different from

Conversely,

Whereas

Unlike what I have just said,

On the one hand,

On the other hand,

2.6 Principles of Outlining

The main function of an outline is to represent the organization of your speech. Thus, your outline should clearly depict your speech's introduction, body, and conclusion and the main points, subpoints, and transitions that support and tie together each of its main parts. For the same reasons that you develop a preliminary thesis statement, you should create a working outline to help you collect and organize your research material. This working outline should contain potential main points, supporting evidence, and introductory, transitional, and concluding statements. Once you have collected and analyzed your evidence, you should begin formulating your thesis statement and organizing your ideas into an outline, and then, if necessary, into a manuscript. When developing your outline, continually verify that its parts remain consistent with your thesis statement, that each part relates clearly to the part before and after it, and that the whole speech is moving toward your intended conclusion. Use the following principles to help you construct your outline or prepare your manuscript. For examples of both speech outlines and manuscripts, consult the Appendix.

1   Design your outline or manuscript so that it is easy to read when you are delivering your speech.

To avoid any problems that may occur with shuffling note cards, type your outline on a standard 8.5-by-11 inch sheet of paper.

To help you read your outline more easily, use an enlarged and bold font, and add extra line spacing. Similarly, when constructing a manuscript, you may want to use a fourteen-point font and double- or triple-space your pages. These design techniques make it easier for you to find your place in your speech's text after making eye contact with your audience. You also may want to use capital letters, different font types and sizes, and underlining to help you recognize the important elements in your text.

You also should consider creating large margins on either side of your text so that you can make any necessary last-minute changes or add notes to remind you of important delivery techniques. For example, if you talk too quickly, write "slow down" and "pause" in the margins to remind you to speak more slowly.

Finally, be sure to number each page so that you can easily rearrange your pages if they become disorganized. Place your title page and bibliography on separate pages so that you can set them aside when speaking.

2   Clearly distinguish between the main parts of your speech and between your main points, subpoints, and sub-subpoints.

The primary function of an outline is to demarcate the main parts of your speech and show the relationship among your points. Making these distinctions clear will help you write and deliver your speech. To help you distinguish between the main parts of your speech, follow these standard rules of outlining:

- Use Roman numerals to indicate the main parts of your speech, and designate them by name (e.g., "I. Introduction," "II. Body," and "III. Conclusion").

- Represent any transitions by separating them with an extra line, by indenting or italicizing them, or by naming them (e.g., "Transition:").

- Indicate main points with capital letters (e.g., "A.," "B.," "C.").

- Identify subpoints by indenting and using Arabic numbers (e.g., "1.," "2.," "3.").

- Designate sub-subpoints by indenting twice and using lower-case letters (e.g., "a.," "b.," "c.").

If your approach to a topic does not lend itself to this traditional style of outlining, create your own outline format. However, remember to use various symbols consistently when representing the different elements of your speech.

3   Use your outline to reflect a clear symmetrical relationship among your speech's various parts.

In general, each of your main points should have approximately the same number of subpoints, and each subpoint should have relatively the same number of sub-subpoints. By following this rule, you place the same emphasis and allot the same amount of time to congruent points. This technique enhances your speech's organizational structure and helps your audience differentiate your main points from your subpoints.

In general, when outlining a main point, make sure it has at least two subpoints. If a main point has fewer than two subpoints, consider making it into a subpoint of another main point, or eliminate it altogether. An exception to this rule is when you want to restate quickly some standard historical facts or operational procedures.

Subpoints should have no more than four sub-subpoints. If a subpoint has more than four sub-subpoints, consider making it into a main point. A possible exception to this rule is when your sub-subpoints consist of a list of items that you will discuss briefly.

4   Use each main point to discuss a different issue relating to your topic.

Your main points should not repeat one another; that is, they should be mutually exclusive. However, to make your speech coherent, you will need to establish some relationship between successive points. This coherence can be maintained effectively with strong transitional statements.

5   Use a combination of complete sentences, short phrases, and separate words in your outline.

Although a general rule of outlining holds that you should use a consistent grammatical form throughout your outline, it is often more effective to use different grammatical forms to represent different components of your speech. Since the content and organization of your speech are important, consider writing your main points and transitional statements as complete sentences. You may even want to use parallel sentences for all of your main points and transitions. This technique serves a variety of functions: it helps you recall your ideas more quickly; it provides a logical symmetry to your speech; and it allows you to identify the main parts of your speech more easily.

When outlining your subpoints, consider when you should use full sentences (as in the case of quotations), and when you should use short phrases for explanations, descriptions, and narratives so that you are forced to discuss them more extemporaneously. In addition, consider when you should represent your sub-subpoints with a single word. A single-word reference will help you recall the idea while reminding you to limit your discussion of it.

6   **Place your oral citations within your outline, and place a bibliography of your sources at the end of your outline.**

To make sure you use oral citations when necessary, place the reference next to the evidence drawn from the source. You must also provide a bibliography of your sources at the end of your outline. If your instructor does not designate what particular notational system to use for either your citations or bibliography, find one that best suits your needs, and follow it throughout your speech. Two widely used styles of documentation are the Chicago style (see *The Chicago Manual of Style,* Fourteenth Edition) and the Modern Language Association (MLA) style (see the *MLA Handbook for Writers of Research Papers,* Fifth Edition). Examples of these two styles follow.

Chicago Style

Books

Book by one author
Loewen, James M. 1996. <u>Lies my teacher told me:</u> <u>Everything your American history textbook got</u> <u>wrong</u>. New York: Simon & Schuster.

Book by two or more authors
Shulman, James L., and William G. Brown. 2000. <u>The game of life: College sports and educational</u> <u>values</u>. Princeton, NJ: Princeton University Press.

Edited book
Sora, Joseph, ed. 1998. <u>Corporate power in the</u> <u>United States</u>. New York: H.W. Wilson.

Chapter or article in an anthology

Anderson, Christopher. 2000. Disneyland. In <u>Television: The critical view</u>. 6th ed. edited by Horace Newcomb. New York: Oxford University Press.

Periodicals

Newspaper article by one author

Rogers, Terry. 1997. "Taking a stand against pollution." <u>San-Diego Union-Tribune</u>, 17 October, A1, A27.

Anonymous newspaper article

"The public school emergency." <u>New York Times</u>, 14 November 2000, A30.

Article from a news periodical by one author

Check, Erika. 2000. "Monkeying around with the brain." <u>Newsweek</u> 136(27 November) 76.

Journal article

Craig, Richard. 2000. "Expectations and elections: How television defines campaign news." <u>Critical Studies in Mass Communication</u> 17, no. 1: 28-44.

Other Sources

Government document

U.S. Department of Commerce. 1992. <u>Workers with Low Earnings, 1964 to 1990</u>. Washington, D.C.: GPO.

Published interview

Jagger, Bianca. "Bianca Jagger: Eyewitness to Murder." Interview by Nancy Collins. In <u>George</u> 5(November 2000): 86-89, 96-100.

Interview that you conducted

Brown, Wendy. Interview by author. Atlanta, Ga,
    1 September 2000.

Article from web site

Ritter, Bill. 2000. "Sniffing Out a Mate," in
    ABCNEWS.com [web site], 27 March 1998. [cited
    15 September 2000]. http://204.202.137.110/sections/
    living/DailyNews/pulse_sexsmells0328.html.

MLA Style

Books

Book by one author

Loewen, James M. Lies My Teacher Told Me: Every-
    thing Your American History Textbook Got Wrong.
    New York: Simon & Schuster, 1996.

Book by two or more authors

Shulman, James L., and William G. Brown. The Game
    of Life: College Sports and Educational Values.
    Princeton: Princeton University Press, 2000.

Edited book

Sora, Joseph, ed. Corporate Power in the United
    States. New York: H.W. Wilson, 1998.

Chapter or article in an anthology

Anderson, Christopher. "Disneyland." Television:
    The Critical View. 6th ed. Ed. Horace Newcomb.
    New York: Oxford University Press, 2000. 17-33.

Periodicals

Newspaper article by one author

Rogers, Terry. "Taking a Stand Against Pollution."
    San-Diego Union-Tribune 17 Oct. 1997, late
    ed.: A1+.

Anonymous newspaper article
"The Public School Emergency." <u>New York Times</u>
14 November 2000: A30.

Article from a news periodical by one author
Check, Erika. "Monkeying Around with the Brain."
<u>Newsweek</u> 27 November 2000: 76.

Journal article
Craig, Richard. "Expectations and Elections: How
Television Defines Campaign News." <u>Critical
Studies in Mass Communication</u> 17 (2000): 28-44.

Other sources

Government document
United States. Dept. of Commerce. <u>Workers with Low
Earnings, 1964 to 1990</u>. Washington: GPO, 1992.

Published interview
Jagger, Bianca. "Bianca Jagger: Eyewitness to
Murder." Interview with Nancy Collins. <u>George</u>
(November, 2000): 86-89, 96-100.

Interview that you conducted
Brown, Wendy. Personal interview. 1 September 2000.

Article from web site
Ritter, Bill. "Sniffing Out a Mate." <u>ABCNEWS.com</u>
27 Mar. 1998. 15 Sept. 2000 <http://204.202.137.110/
sections/living/DailyNews/pulse_sexsmells0328.html>

APA Style

Books

A book with one author
Rodriguez, R. (1982). *A hunger of memory: The
education of Richard Rodriguez*. Boston: Godine.

A book with two to six authors
Nesselroade, J.R., & Baltes, P.B. (1999). *Longitudinal research in the study of behavioral development.* New York: Academic Press.

A book with an editor
Dohrenwend, B.S. & Dohrenwend, B.P. (Eds.). (1999). *Stressful life events: Their nature and effects.* New York: Wiley.

A book with a translator
Trajan, P.D. (1927). *Psychology of animals.* (H. Simone, Trans.) Washington, DC: Halperin.

A book with no author or an anonymous book
Merriam-Webster's collegiate dictionary (11th ed.). (2003). Springfield, MA: Merriam-Webster.
For a work whose author is actually given as "Anonymous," use this word in place of the author's name and alphabetize it as if it were a name.

A later edition
Bolinger, D.L. (1975). *Aspects of language* (2nd ed.). New York: Harcourt Brace Jovanovich.

An article in a magazine
Talbot, M. (2004, August 9). The bad mother. *The New Yorker,* 40-46.

An article in a newspaper
Kolata, G. (2004, January 7). Kill all the bacteria! *The New York Times,* pp. B1, B3

An article in an online journal
Wissink, J.A. (2000). Techniques of smoking cessation among teens and adults. *Adolescent Medicine, 2.* Retrieved August 16, 2004, from http://www.easu.edu/AdolescentMedicine/2-Wissink.html

A journal article from an electronic database

Wilkins, J.M. (1999). The myths of the only child.
   Psychology Update 11(1), 16-23. Retrieved
   December 20, 2004, from ProQuest Direct database.

An entire web site (text citation)

The APA's Web site provides answers to frequently
   asked questions about style
   (http://www.apa.org).
Cite an entire Web site (rather than a specific
page or document) by giving the electronic address
in your text.

3

The Nature of the Exordium

The principal function of the exordium is to put the listeners into a proper frame of mind so that they will want to hear what the speaker has to say. Obviously, the speaker's first concern must be challenging the attention of his listeners, for whatever he says without their attention will be lost. Next, he must gain their respect before they will accept his message. Further, he should find the *common ground* between his audience and himself. If these steps are followed, the inevitable questions that arise in the listeners' minds will be answered. Until they are answered, the audience will not be ready to hear the speaker's message. The speaker should take, therefore, as much time as is needed to accomplish these steps before moving into the last part of the exordium, which is introducing the subject of his speech. This step should not be confused with stating his position; he should commit himself to a position only at the psychologically appropriate moment. But, after the initial matters of adjustment have been satisfied, the audience will begin to ask, "What is he going to talk about?" Generally, a designation of the speech topic will suffice at this point, and the position can be presented later.

In a sense the exordium is a grand transition. The speaker has the job of focusing the diverse thoughts of his audience (each member probably is thinking of something different at the onset of the speech) on one focal point. Then, after getting the audience to think in unison on some point, he can shift its thinking to the subject of his speech. All of this is done while gaining their trust and helping them to adjust to him.

The speaker who moves hurriedly through the exordium, treating it as a mere formality or a stylistic necessity, is building into the speaking situation distractions that will interfere with his ability to hold attention later in the speech. The exordium conditions the audience's psychological readiness, and it should not be left until that readiness to listen to the speaker's case is accomplished.

Attention, ethos, and identification are of great importance in the exordium, but their usefulness continues throughout the speech. Because they are developed at the beginning of the speech, they will be treated in detail in the present chapter. Care should be taken to ensure their continuing function in the remainder of the speech.

3.1 Challenging the Attention

1   Attention defined.

Picture a large auditorium where an audience is congregating to hear a featured speaker. Think of the many subjects occupying the thoughts of the people as they assemble: One may be estimating the number of people arriving while he sits in the audience; he may look about and admire the interior decoration of the auditorium. Another may be wondering what the speaker will look like, or recalling what the newspaper said about the speaker's experiences. And still another may have his thoughts farther afield—wondering whether he can get his work report on the boss's desk on time tomorrow, or whether his client will keep an appointment on Thursday. Probably not one is so absorbed in his thoughts that he would fail to stand up to let someone take the seat next to him. All are vaguely aware of what is going on around them, but their thoughts are centered on some specific area. Their fields of awareness thus encompass more than their center of attention. One part of their fields of awareness occupies their minds most, while the rest becomes background.

The familiar illustration of faces and a vase shows that when one focuses on a specific feature of a field its other parts become background. If you look at the vase in **Figure 3.1**, the faces tend to fade into the background and vice versa. So it is with the people in the audience;

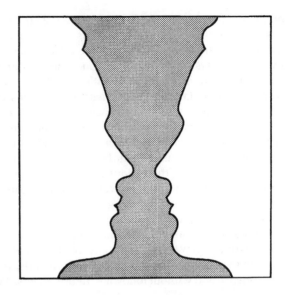

FIGURE 3.1. *Figure-ground.*

certain parts of their fields of awareness become *figure* (or maximally clear to them), while others become *ground* (or relatively less clear).

One additional example may clarify the nature of attention in terms of figure and ground. Mark, a two-and-one-half-year-old child, was shown a field of one hundred lima beans. Ten groups of ten beans had been numbered from 1 to 10 and had been shuffled so that they were in random order. He was instructed to pick out all of the beans with the number 7 on them and to place them in a cup. For each correct response he was given a reward in the form of a raisin; incorrect responses won no reward. For the first few trials, his responses were very slow; he would look at each bean and either accept or reject it. Within a short time, however, he was able to focus his attention on the one number he was looking for, so that it stood out more clearly than all of the others. Soon he could pick them up and put them into the cup as quickly as he could move. The stimulus beans had become figure and the others within the field had become ground. The fact that the figure beans produced reinforcement (reward) is of significance here also. Attention is attracted to phenomena that reward or promise to reward the observer.

When the intended background becomes more rewarding than the intended figure, one is said to be distracted. That is, one's attention is focused on the wrong parts of the field of awareness. Indeed, some attempts have been made to develop tests of attention ability through the use of distractions. One such test consists of a number of questions whose answers are obvious to anyone who pays attention—questions such as "Who is buried in Grant's tomb?" or "What day follows Tuesday?" Simultaneously, limericks with clever twists are presented. Those subjects who are distracted by the limericks are paying insufficient attention to the questions to answer them.

When the speaker in our hypothetical speaking situation finally comes onto the stage and begins to speak, he is immediately faced with the problem of subordinating the various thoughts of his listeners so that they become background and his words become figure. Out of courtesy or curiosity, audiences usually give the speaker a chance to challenge their interest, but if he is too slow in doing it, they will become distracted. The speaker's first and continuing job, then, is to make his words more rewarding than any of the many possible distractors in the situation. Unless the audience attends, it cannot follow his arguments, and without following the arguments, it will not become persuaded.

Because the ability to challenge the attention is a prime requisite of a persuasive speaker, the student of persuasive speaking should study the factors that compel attention until he develops a sensitivity to attention feedback and a mastery of the techniques for securing and holding attention.

3.2 Factors Compelling Attention

The Vital.   Most attention is related in some way to security. This generalization is seen most clearly in the vital role of the basic needs. Anything that threatens our physical welfare—our friends or loved ones, our pride—or, conversely, anything that promises to satisfy our basic needs will compel our attention. To the seasick sailor who is back to normal after having been unable to eat for a week, any conversation on the food specialties of the next port will attract his interest. Or an apathetic public, normally disinterested in civil defense measures, will find its attention involuntarily focused on first aid courses and the like when its safety is threatened by a declaration of war. Has not every college student at some time or another found his mind wandering from the lecture but quickly returning to it when in the background he hears the instructor say, "... and you may find some reference to this concept on your next quiz"?

Appeals to the vital almost inevitably compel attention, but if such dramatic appeals are not followed up with sufficient justification, a resentment is established against the speaker. Too frequently do novice persuasive speakers rely on this means of gaining attention only to find that their follow-up is inappropriate for the amount of tension aroused. The resentment then becomes the dominant factor in the listener's mind and it becomes a distraction.

The Expection-Observation Differential. Anything that fails to coincide with what is expected tends to attract attention, also. Our expectations provide us with a certain sense of security. If we can predict with fair accuracy what is going to happen, our fear of the unknown is reduced. However, when our predictions are interrupted, our security is threatened, and we involuntarily focus our attention on the unexpected cause of the interruption.

How often have you sat in a restaurant without noticing the background dinner music? Now, if you were touring abroad and found yourself in a French restaurant with French dinner music playing you likely would not notice it either until a familiar American song was played. Then your attention would probably be focused sharply on the music. The familiar among strange surroundings is not expected. Conversely, have you ever walked into your room and had your attention immediately focused on your desk where someone had left an unfamiliar book for you? The unusual among familiar surroundings stands out because it is unexpected.

Humor illustrates the compelling nature of the differences between what is suspected and what is actually observed. Almost any funny story begins in such a way as to "lead you on." You begin to visualize a situation in which the protagonist is headed toward some disappointment or tragedy, but just before the grave consequences materialize (and you fully expect them to materialize) the storyteller inserts a quick "twist" of events so that the tragedy is avoided (and your observation is at variance with your expectation). Grimes, illustrating this concept, explains **Figure 3.2** by saying:

How can BCD occur in a joke? Suppose we look at this one:
LAWYER *(to opponent):* "You're the biggest damn fool in the city."
JUDGE *(rapping for order):* "Gentlemen! You forget I am here."

In this courtroom altercation the movement starts with the lawyer's angry thrust at his opponent, which we shall call AB, the judge's reprimand is BC, and D is the point of quick realization of what the judge has *actually* said. The movement toward reprimand leads the listener to expect such a phrase as, "This is a court of justice," or "You forget where you are." If the judge had ruled the lawyer out of order with either of those phrases, the movement of the incident would have gone smoothly unimpeded to D, and there would have been no BCD. As it is [sic], the judge's admission that he is the biggest damn fool in

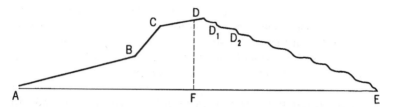

FIGURE 3.2   *The* course *or* process *aspects of the experience. AE— hypothetical base line of experience; event (time and space). ABCDF–cognitive aspect (perceptual part of pattern; dynamic stimulus field). A–beginning. E–end. AD–unfolding (or developing) movement. AB–tension develops. BC–tension mounts (any sudden change of direction). CD–tension holds, sharpens unexpected resolution and insight that complete the cognitive aspect of the D experience. D–experience, accompanied by shock and sometimes (always) by surprise. DFE–mirth. BCD–governed by events (including language events) classified as incongruous. D_1–surprise. D_2–relief. (After Wilma H. Grimes, "A Theory of Humor for Public Address: The Mirth Experience,"* Speech Monographs, *August, 1955, p. 220. Used by permission.)*

the city comes as a "shock" to the listener (as it might have to the judge). AB might be interpreted as "angry lawyer deserving a squelch from dignified, perhaps pompous judge," and moving toward it with angry words. BCD becomes "unexpected degradation of the judge" instead of "expected degradation of the lawyer."

Shock and suspense both are produced, essentially because of differences between what is observed and what is expected; their capacities to attract or to hold attention are obvious. Although they each gain attraction properties from the expectation-observation differential, they differ essentially in their application of it. Shock occurs when a door slams unexpectedly; that is, when a sudden observation occurs without having been anticipated. But suspense develops when what appears to be inevitable does not materialize as expected. The speaker may use both devices for attention control, but suspense usually holds attention longer than shock.

The Varied.   To illustrate the importance of variety in sustaining attention, repeat the word *complicated* one hundred times as rapidly as you can. Notice that before you finish, the word becomes distorted. The reason is that nerve fatigue and the behavioral phenomenon of habituation (repeatedly unrewarded responses) cause interference with your ability to concentrate on what you are saying. Likewise, an unvaried vocal pattern, an unvaried language usage, or an unvaried bodily response tends to produce a monotony or boredom that destroys attention. Particularly in the delivery aspects of a speech, but also in stylistic, developmental, and arrangement aspects, variety or change is important for keeping the listener's mind focused on the speech.

Few people recognize the role of variation in holding attention as clearly as musicians, who change the key, the tempo, the rhythm, the volume, or instrumentation. Thus, an arranger can repeat a simple motif throughout an entire number without its becoming monotonous.

The Conflicting. Can you name a single novel, short story, or play you have read that held your interest in which there was not a conflict inherent in the plot? Some kind of conflict almost inevitably appears: It may be a conflict between man and nature, between men, between man and society, or between man and himself, but a conflict there is because conflicts hold attention. Even the symphonic composer pits one theme against another so that they compete, struggle, and attempt to gain dominance over each other.

If, therefore, a speaker can involve his listeners in a conflict (either directly or emphatically), he will probably hold their attention, unless the conflict becomes too great and its resolution too vital. Some evidence is available to suggest that if the conflict creates too much anxiety, the effectiveness of the speech will be reduced. Hovland, Janis, and Kelley state: ". . . observations of reactions to intense anxiety stimuli suggest that when emotional tension is strongly aroused, distractibility tendencies are increased and cognitive functions tend to be temporarily impaired. If this were to occur when a strong threat appeal is presented in a persuasive communication, there would be less attention and less learning of the content, which would result in lowered effectiveness."

By relating another's conflict vividly, the audience may experience the conflict emphatically, as in this example from Jack London's short story "To Build a Fire." A north woodsman, having consumed more than enough at the village tavern, began a lengthy walk to his cabin in the woods. His "inner glow" prevented his awareness of the dangerous subzero weather until he had reached the point of no return. Finally recognizing that he would freeze if he continued his journey, he set about to build a fire for warmth. With his stiff, awkward fingers he crumbled the tinder and painstakingly placed first twigs then larger sticks into position. A numbed search through his pockets yielded only two wooden matches. With utmost care, he shielded one match with his aching hand while attempting to strike it with the other. It flared, flickered, and died. He was sufficiently sober now to recognize his reduced chances for survival. Cautiously, almost lovingly, he struck the last match. It flickered once; it flickered again; then it caught. He sighed briefly when the tinder began to ignite. While blowing as gently as a panicked man can control his blowing, he heard the twigs begin to crackle; he saw the flames licking around the larger sticks. After a deep, heavy sigh—a secure sigh—he began to feed larger limbs to the fire. Now he could relax and warm himself. He was safe. Just as he was about to rearrange the sticks, he blinked not believing what he saw. The fire was out. The heat from his lifesaving fire had melted the snow on the pine branch above it. The resulting avalanche smothered his fire and, consequently, his life.

Even more effective than an emphatic conflict is an actual conflict created within the listeners' minds. By pitting two equally strong, yet antagonistic, attitudes held by the listener against each other, a sense of instability or a nagging unsettled feeling will compel the mind to search for a way of resolving the conflict. The attention will be directed toward regaining stability.

A study was conducted that supports this conclusion. A large number of college students was asked to complete attitude scales designed to measure the direction and strength of attitudes toward socialism and unionism. Each student then heard a tape-recorded speech that attempted to create conflicts among them. An examination of one of the conflicts will suffice for our present purposes. Those listeners who held very unfavorable attitudes toward both socialism and unionism experienced an avoidance-avoidance conflict as they heard the speech. That is, the reasoning of the speech demanded that, although neither alternative was desirable, they ultimately choose either a greater degree of socialism or a greater degree of unionism. They were forced logically to select one or the other of two undesirable solutions.

Immediately after hearing the speech all the students were given a retention test covering the material presented in the speech. Those students who had been exposed to the avoidance-avoidance conflict were significantly superior in remembering the details of the speech to any other people tested. The inference drawn was that the superior retention of the avoidance-avoidance conflict group was produced by the conflict. There had been some concern that if the conflict were too strong, the opposite reaction might occur. But Hovland, Janis, and Kelley have referred to an experiment designed to test this hypothesis and concluded that ". . . the evidence concerning the amount of information acquired from the communication did not indicate that the strong appeal produced inattentiveness or any form of distraction that would interfere with learning efficiency during the communication session."

The Challenging.   Often, attention may be attracted by a challenge, a dare, or a strong suggestion. The challenge may be subtle, but that is not essential. Here is a challenge for the reader; all of its sublety is stripped away: Try, for thirty seconds not to think of a polar bear. The challenge not to think of it will force your attention the more strongly toward it.

Similarly, if a speaker has a point he wants the husbands in the audience to pay particular attention to, he may use negative suggestion by saying, "Now this next item is intended for the wives in the audience. You husbands just think of something else for a moment because I want to let the women in on a little secret about how we men think." What is the effect? It is obvious: The men listen with keen interest.

The Concrete. Concreteness intensifies the imagery, and the more vivid mental images are (that is, the more they appeal to particular senses), the more they compel attention. The factor causing this differential focus was the use of concrete references as opposed to generalities. When the listener is actively engaged in imagining a specific situation, his mind is not likely to stray.

3.3 Establishing Ethos and Identification

After the speaker has collected the divergent thoughts of his listeners and all are thinking about the same thing, his next important task in preparing them for his message is to gain their confidence. Until they feel that they can trust him to work for their best interest, nagging doubts will distract their attention from what he is saying. Their attention will, therefore, be more effectively controlled if the speaker eliminates the most probable distractions before moving on into his case. The understanding of two concepts, ethos and identification, will thus aid the speaker.

3.4 Definitions

Ethos. Ethos is a probative force drawn from the speaker himself. It may be thought of as the image the audience holds of the speaker. The terms *prestige* and *credibility* are often used to clarify the meaning of ethos. This image, which is inevitably formed, is determined chiefly by the audience's estimation of the speaker's intelligence, his character, and the degree of good will he appears to have for his listeners.

Many factors (too many to enumerate) contribute to the making of an image: prior reputation; an air of confidence in voice, dress, and bodily activity; a command of the subject and of the language; keenness of reasoning and sensitivity to feelings. All of these and many more provide the substance from which the speaker's ethos is determined. Audiences may also formulate their images on the bases of who sponsors the speaker or who the speaker holds in high esteem.

A report of an experimental study on the effect of ethos will help to demonstrate its usefulness to the persuasive speaker.[6] Three equated groups were asked to listen to the same recorded speech. In one group the speech was attributed to the Surgeon General of the United States; in another group it was attributed to the Secretary of the Communist Party in America; and in the third group it was attributed to a college sophomore. Ballots were given to each member of each group both before and after the speech was presented so that a change of opinion might be measured. As was to be expected, the alleged speaker with the greatest ethos (the Surgeon General) was able to shift opinion significantly more than the other alleged speakers, even though the identical speech was played to all three groups.

Although the Haiman study has become a classic in experimental literature, many other studies on ethos have been conducted. Anderson and Clevenger have summarized the experimental literature on ethos; some of their generalizations are worthy of note for our purposes.

3.5 Methods of Achieving Ethos and Identification

Deserve the respect of your audience. Quintilian considered the ethical behavior of the speaker to be of such importance that he endorsed Marcus Cato's concept and defined the orator as "a good man, is skilled in speaking." Quintilian was not merely moralizing; he was convinced that persuasion requires the audience's respect, and that the audience's respect is more easily and more consistently achieved when the speaker is sincere, careful in his analysis, and genuinely concerned with the welfare of his listeners. The speaker's effect is nonverbal as well as verbal, and when attitudes of contempt and motives of selfish manipulation are manifested nonverbally, no amount of lip service to the contrary will be accepted. Thus, the saying "What you are speaks so loudly that I cannot hear what you say."

Lincoln was fond of telling a story applicable to the point that it is, practically, easier to be respectable than to appear respectable. He asserted that it is easier to tell the truth, because lying requires that you remember all of your lies so that you do not later contradict yourself. Likewise, it is better to possess the qualities that enhance ethos than to play the role.

Take the time to gain the respect of your audience. Some people find it extremely difficult to refer to their qualifications or to their strength of character; others have no such difficulty. Either extreme is detrimental to the speaker, for if he makes no attempt to develop ethos, he weakens his chances of success; but if he is too boastful he will antagonize his listeners. Ethos development should be subtle, but should be accomplished.

Often, the person who introduces the speaker can do much by way of gaining respect for him. The speaker may well ask that certain information be used in introducing him, but he should avoid such glowing introductions that he is an anticlimax.

One senator recently established himself as an authority on the Cuban crisis through the subtle reference to his firsthand inspection tour. Rather than say, "Now look here, I've just come from Cuba and I know what is going on there," he took time to develop a brief narrative. He said that as he got off the plane in Havana the week before, he was met by several Cubans who were eager to tell their story. They guided him on extensive tours, they arranged for him to talk to Castro, and so forth. Subtly, he was telling the audience that he knew what he was talking about, but he was doing it in a way that was not obnoxious.

Taking the time to identify with the audience's goals and wishes is an even more subtle and often more effective method of enhancing ethos. This takes time that might otherwise be spent on a more detailed development of the case, but in the long run, it is time well spent.

Strive to achieve a Mature Personality Adjustment. In Chapter 4 several types of personalities are described. The most effective personality type for good communication (and this does not suggest that all speakers should conform to a fixed pattern) has a realistic sense of confidence in his own beliefs and abilities. At the same time he has a healthy respect for the dignity and the abilities of his listeners. If his confidence is low on either of these dimensions, it will be expressed in ways of which he is unaware, and his ethos will suffer accordingly.

Put yourself in the position of your listeners during the analysis stage. There are very few, if any, one-sided subjects suitable for persuasion. If you can understand your listeners' positions, even though you may disagree with them, such understanding will enable you to identify more closely with them. It is even possible that after such an understanding, you may elect not to persuade them.

Find and stress your common ground. Because your attitude and the attitude of your audience may differ, it does not mean that there is no common meeting ground. Your audience may disagree with you that federal aid to education is desirable. That is, they may agree that equal opportunity for education is desirable, or if not that, on the next level of abstraction that mass education is desirable. Somewhere there must be a common ground even though it is on a very abstract level. The speaker should find the most concrete level of agreement on the abstraction ladder. If, as a matter of course, he tries to identify at too high an abstraction level, his appeals will normally be based on "God, Mother, and flag." In some cases this level may be the only one where common ground exists, but if more concrete levels are available his task is made easier by beginning with them.

Every opportunity to stress the points of agreement in feelings, interests, beliefs, and experiences should be considered, and at the same time all points of disagreement should be minimized. A debater seeks to point up the differences in position, but a persuasive speaker strives to minimize them. When an open conflict between positions is inevitable, utmost tact should be used. For instance, let the words of others express your thoughts if they are harsh. The use of a proverb or other quotation puts the emphasis on conflicting ideas rather than on conflicting personalities. Another bit of tact can be followed by telling of your dislike of certain faults in others rather than expressing your dislike of that particular fault in your listeners. You stand in a better light when you are able to criticize an idea while preserving the ego. Finally, by praising a person for avoiding certain of his shortcomings instead of criticizing him for them when he does commit them, you may make your position known without antagonism.

When the speaker is certain that he has established rapport with his audience, he is then ready to introduce the topic of his speech.

4

Delivery, Part 1

4.1 Modes of Delivery

Listed below are the four main modes of delivering a speech. Study each mode to determine which best suits your topic, delivery style, and speech situation. If time permits, try different modes of delivery when practicing your speech. Practicing these different delivery modes will both improve your delivery skills and increase your familiarity with your speech's text.

1   Extemporaneous delivery.

An extemporaneous delivery is given from an outline. It is the most common delivery mode because it offers you the chance to refer to an outline of your speech while allowing you to choose your words, construct your sentences, and vary your appeals when delivering your speech. Thus by speaking extemporaneously you can maintain a healthy balance between presenting your speech's text and modifying your delivery to fit the needs of your audience.

The other main advantages of an extemporaneous delivery are that it allows for increased eye contact and the ability to adapt your speech to your audience's nonverbal feedback. For instance, you can rephrase an explanation or provide an additional example when your audience appears confused, embellish an emotional appeal once you recognize its initial impact, or eliminate a point if you are running out of time. Its main disadvantages are that it requires a great deal of preparation to make your main points flow together smoothly, and you must know when to speak from your outline and when to talk more directly to your audience. You also must avoid the temptation of trying to memorize an exact set of words, phrases, or statements that sound good when you are practicing your speech, for you may stumble or repeat yourself needlessly when trying to recall your ideas.

2   Manuscript delivery.

The manuscript delivery is most often used in speeches where stating your position, providing definitive evidential support, and wording your statements correctly are of utmost importance. As its name indicates, this mode of delivery is given from a written text that contains your whole speech.

While a manuscript explicitly sets forth all of your ideas, it limits your ability to adapt your speech to your audience's nonverbal feedback. As such, a manuscript delivery provides little opportunity for you to relay additional information, rephrase a confusing statement, or omit ineffective ideas. A manuscript delivery also may cause you to limit your eye contact and speak too quickly, and it may cause you to neglect other verbal and nonverbal delivery techniques. To avoid many of these pitfalls, refrain from simply reading your speech, speak slowly, and pronounce your words clearly. Likewise, remember to vary your tone, use facial expression and gesture effectively, and make eye contact with your audience whenever possible.

3   Impromptu delivery.

Like improvisational theater, an impromptu delivery is unprepared and unrehearsed. It usually entails no research and uses neither an outline nor a manuscript.

The advantage of an impromptu delivery is that it is more informal and allows you to maintain eye contact with your audience. Moreover, it can highlight your knowledge of your topic and your sincerity. At the same time, however, it can expose your ignorance about your topic. Your lack of preparation also can make it difficult for you to state your thesis clearly, organize your speech and its main points adequately, present evidence thoroughly, and refer your sources properly. To avoid these problems, find places in your speech to restate your thesis statement and use review transitions to help you remember your main points.

4.2 Elements of Vocal Delivery

It is easy to recognize how your vocal delivery plays a major role in the way you present yourself to your audience. Like your style, your delivery also is integral to the meaning you convey. Your vocal delivery is not just a way to embellish or ornament your ideas; rather, it plays a major role in how you communicate your ideas and, consequently, how your audience will comprehend and interpret them. Moreover, your delivery can help your audience follow your speech's overall organization and increase the appeal of your proofs. To learn more about how to deliver your speech, study the elements of vocal and nonverbal delivery given here and in the next section.

1   Register.

Your **register** is the range of pitch, rate, volume, pauses, and enunciation used when delivering a speech. When giving a speech, try to stay within your **middle range,** which is somewhere between a conversational and formal style of speaking. Your middle range should fit naturally with your voice and personality. Your delivery style and personal demeanor should be somewhat more formal than they are in conversation, but not artificial, affected, or pretentious. Your tone should be a degree lower than your conversational voice; your speed, a degree slower; your volume, a degree higher; your pauses, a degree longer; and your enunciation, a degree clearer (see the following subsections).

While keeping your delivery within this middle range, use **vocal variety** to avoid a monotone delivery. That is, alter your speed, volume, tone, and pauses to reflect the different elements of your speech. For instance, cue your introduction and conclusion by using the same tone of voice, adopt a slightly lower tone and slower speed when stating your main definitions and explanations, and then speak more quickly and raise your pitch when relating an example or humorous anecdote. When presenting well-known facts or a short story, speak more quickly and in a light, conversational manner. For longer narratives, remember to use vocal variety to move your audience through the various stages of the story and the emotions you are attempting to evoke. Within a narrative, also try to depict hurried and fraught action by increasing your speed while representing more everyday or orderly actions with a slower, more methodical pace.

Vocal variety can also help you convey feeling and mood. For instance, if you want to instill a sense of anticipation and excitement about your subject, speak louder and more quickly, use greater changes in your inflection, and increase your gesturing. To reflect the serious nature of your subject, start and finish your speech in a more subdued manner, and use facial gesturing to reflect your sincerity and concern. Likewise, when warning or advising your audience about a serious matter, attempting to solicit pity, or expressing fear or shame, lower your tone, speak more slowly, and pause longer and more often. On the other hand, when arguing vehemently or placing blame on a culprit, raise your tone, increase your speed, and pause only for punctuation and to give your audience a chance to recognize the severity of the individual's ideas or actions.

2   Tone.

In music, pitch and tone are often used interchangeably, whereas in speech, your voice's tone is equated with your voice **inflection**. Your **tone** denotes the highness or lowness of your voice. By raising or lowering your tone, you can convey a variety of meanings. For instance, consider lowering your tone to suggest an implied meaning, stress an important fact, or express a sincere conviction. You can also raise your tone when citing an example or telling a personal story.

You may want to change your inflection to stress certain words or phrases. For example, use your tone to reflect the meaning of words such as *devote, caring, hateful,* and *patriotic*. Similarly, words and phrases that express the urgency of a situation, such as "the time is now" or "without hesitation," should be spoken quickly and forcefully, whereas those expressing a long, deliberate process, such as "after years of soul-searching" or "he moved cautiously," should be stated more slowly.

You also should repeat the same patterns of inflection when expressing similar ideas or parallel statements, and change your inflection to represent contrasting ideas in antithetical statements such as "To err is human, to forgive is divine."

3   Rate.

The **rate** of your delivery refers to how quickly you are speaking. Although most people normally speak at a rate of 125 to 150 words per minute, slow down your rate when delivering a speech so that your audience can comprehend your ideas more easily.

How you vary your rate and pauses establishes the **rhythm** or **flow** of your delivery. Creating an effective rhythm demands maintaining some consistency as well as varying your speed (and other vocal elements), punctuating sentences and phrases with short pauses, and using your speed to indicate parts of your speech. As a general rule, speak more slowly at the beginning of your speech so that your audience can adjust to your delivery. You should also slow your rate when stressing important points, abstract explanations, significant facts, or crucial statistics, and increase your rate when presenting familiar examples, figurative analogies, and short narratives. To build excitement in your conclusion and arouse your audience's emotions, move from speaking softly and slowly to speaking more quickly and loudly.

4 Volume.

Your **volume** is how loudly or softly you speak. Within your middle range, always raise your volume to just above your regular conversational voice, and remember to project your voice by bringing air from your diaphragm and chest, rather than just speaking from your throat. Projecting your voice will place less strain on your throat and allow you to be heard by all your audience members.

In general, increase your volume when stressing an important point, making a critical argument, emphasizing a definition, or expressing a strong conviction. Lower your volume when offering a helpful subpoint, expressing an empathic emotion, or building a suspenseful story. In addition, raise or lower your volume to call attention to a word or phrase. You also will want to speak more softly (and slowly) in parts of some speeches, such as a eulogy, and more loudly when delivering parts of other speeches, such as the climactic ending of an introductory speech.

5 Enunciation.

Enunciation entails pronouncing words and sentences properly. The main reason why a speaker mispronounces words is that he or she is speaking too quickly as a result of being nervous. Avoid mispronouncing words by controlling your speech anxiety and by making a conscious effort to slow down and pronounce each part of a word or sentence clearly.

To improve your enunciation, practice pronouncing difficult or commonly mispronounced words. For instance, practice pronouncing words with an *ing* suffix so that you do not leave off the last *g* and make sure to say *want to* and not the slang *wanna*. Similarly, make sure that you are pronouncing short and long vowels properly, such as the *a* in *bat* and *cape;* and soft and hard consonants, such as the *c* in *cap* and *catch*. Another way to ensure that proper pronunciation is to **round the sounds** by exaggerating your mouth's movements when forming a word.

Proper enunciation also involves placing the proper inflection on words and sentences. By changing your inflection, you can change the meaning of a statement. For instance, you can alter the implied answer to the question, "Should we blame the tobacco companies or smokers for the high levels of lung cancer in this country?" by stressing either the words *tobacco companies* or *smokers*. In general, your inflection should be lower at the end of a declarative sentence to reflect its truthfulness, but higher at the end of a question to signify its speculative character. However, questions that begin with an interrogative such as

Why, or imperatives that begin with the command *Never,* should begin with a strong inflection.

Try to avoid several common problems with enunciation. First, do not slur your words or speak too softly at the end of a sentence. These problems usually result from a lack of breath. Hence, remember that the length of a sentence should be no more than the length of one of your breaths, and you should always pause at the end of a sentence. Second, to avoid mispronouncing words, do not string together too many multisyllable words and long sentences. If you are using a long, complex sentence, remember to speak slowly and stress its internal punctuation with pauses. Third, if you are having trouble placing the proper inflection in a sentence, underline the word or phrase written on your outline or manuscript that you need to stress.

With regard to regional dialect, some audience members believe such speech patterns bring character to a speech, whereas others, rightly or wrongly, believe they represent a lack of education or preparation. Thus, you must decide whether and to what degree you should rid your voice of its conversational character or regional flavor. However, you always should avoid such speaking patterns if they cause you to enunciate your words unclearly and make your speech incomprehensible.

6   Pauses.

A **pause** is a brief moment of silence between words, sentences, important points, or parts of your speech. Pauses serve a variety of functions: (1) They indicate grammatical marks that are not evident in an oral medium, such as colons or semicolons; (2) they give your audience an opportunity to consider what you have just said and what you will say next; (3) they allow your audience to absorb the impact of an important point or savor a figure of speech or narrative; (4) they help create a smooth, intelligible rhythm by providing breaks between units of thought such as clauses, phrases, and sentences; and (5) they give you a chance to breathe and collect your thoughts before moving to your next point.

You also should use a longer pause after your introduction and before your conclusion so that your audience can more clearly distinguish the main parts of your speech. Likewise, pause after a rhetorical question to allow your audience time to consider the question's implication. Finally, try to eliminate filler words such as *um, ah,* or *OK* by pausing, collecting your thoughts, and then continuing your sentence.

5

The content of these pages remains accurate and useful in 2005, but even in 1972 when I wrote the revised edition I should have known better than to have addressed my reader as "he," "him," etc. Many public speakers then and many more now are women. Their contributions are made in small, local groups as well as the halls of Congress and world-wide fora. So, please expand the pronouns appropriately to "she," "her," "one," "the speaker," or simply convert to the plural. Best wishes to the women and men in this course.

Jane Blankenship, Ph. D.,
University of Massachusetts,
Amherst, Ma. (2005)

Delivery, Part 2

5.1 The Basic Elements of Good Delivery

In his effort to acquire effective delivery, the speaker should: (1) recognize what good delivery is; (2) observe and evaluate himself objectively; and (3) practice, first to eliminate large problems, then to refine his skill. Let us briefly discuss each stage.

1 Recognize good delivery.

The main way to discover the elements of effective delivery is to observe both poor and good speakers. Try to suggest ways in which they vary. Among the many characteristics of effective delivery, the two major elements are probably directness and force.

Directness. The quality of directness in conversation and in public speaking stems mainly from two sources: (1) a desire to communicate, to exchange opinions, to talk out ideas; and (2) a concentration on the ideas under discussion which allows the speaker to forget himself. Whately has commented: "The practical rule . . . to be adopted . . . is, not only to pay no studied attention to the Voice, but studiously to *withdraw* the thoughts from it, and to dwell as intently as possible on the Sense; trusting to nature to suggest spontaneously the proper emphases and tones."

When the speaker has eliminated all distinct thought of himself, he can concentrate on what he has to say, on his audience, and on the relationship between himself and his audience. He can concentrate on the essential feature of communication, the sharing of an idea, attitude, or opinion. The delivery of most great speakers has been marked by their conversational powers. Consider this comment about the speaking of the great abolitionist orator, Wendell Phillips: "The *character* of his voice—the man in it—had the effect of 'finding' its auditor. It has an *intimate* tone, as if he were speaking to each one as an unknown friend. . . ."

Most people manage, in everyday conversation, to convey their attitudes toward a subject in many ways—tone of voice, word choice, gesture. Why then, when we stand on a platform before an audience to give a speech, should there be a psychological compulsion to repress outward manifestations of interest in a subject we have presumably spent time and work preparing specifically for presentation?

Force. Force is associated with the features often designated as "animation" and "vitality." It stems from a feeling of deep earnestness and communicates to the audience the excitement of a nervous system and a brain working at top form, stimulated by having to think rapidly and aloud, and responding with spontaneity, imagination, and vividness.

Force is motivated by deep interest in the subject. Unless ideas are animated, delivery must necessarily be dull and lifeless. A speaker can experiment with the mechanics of voice and gesture, but they represent no substitute for a strong belief in what one is saying. When beliefs are strong and clearly defined, when the speaker is confident of them, he can rely on them, just as he does in conversation, to convey his feelings and his attitudes about what he is saying. When the speaker has carried over into his public speaking the most desirable qualities of his conversational speaking, he will fully realize the content of his words as he utters them. The force of his ideas will be naturally manifested in forceful delivery.

2   Observe and evaluate your own delivery.

After the beginning speaker has watched and listened to the delivery of other speakers, he should evaluate himself by listening to himself as he speaks, by tape recordings of his own speech, through teacher criticism, and the criticisms of other students in the class. He should check especially for directness of communication (both intellectual directness and physical directness):

1. Is there "vivid-realization-of-idea-at-moment-of-utterance"?
2. Is there eye contact—direct and sustained?
3. Is there bodily responsiveness to what is said?
4. Does pronunciation meet acceptable standards? Is articulation clear?
5. Is there vocal variety in rate, inflection, and volume?

When the student knows what particular areas of delivery need work, he can, with the aid of his teacher, plan exercises designed specifically to help him.

3   Practice to eliminate problems and refine skills.

The next step is to get as much practice as possible by speaking often and always objectively evaluating your own performance. The two basic prerequisites to effective delivery must be remembered: (1) preparedness, and (2) a genuine desire to communicate.

5.2 Special Problems of Beginning Speakers

Beginning public speakers face some special problems in delivering a speech. We shall discuss nine. By exploring the causes of the problems, their remedies will become clearer.

1   Nervousness.

Nervousness should be viewed as a natural phenomenon, almost universally felt in the public speaking situation. The speaker's task is not easy, and some degree of tension serves to remind him of this. Insofar as stage fright is controlled, it is basically helpful. As Walter and Scott point out, certain physical changes take place during stage fright that can aid the speaker. They indicate that the body may obtain more than its usual *energy* under tension because of these changes:

1. More blood sugar, which furnishes energy, is available.
2. Insulin, which increases the permeability of the membrane surrounding the cells to the blood sugar, is secreted, with the result that more food can get inside the cells.
3. Thyroxin, a catalyst that speeds the burning of sugar inside the cells, is added to the blood stream.
4. Blood pressure increases.
5. Respiration increases.
6. The conductivity of nerves increases slightly.
7. More oxygen is available so that more fuel is burned.
8. The poisons from metabolism are removed more speedily so that toxicity and fatigue are reduced.

Thus, the speaker can potentially think more rapidly about his subject when he is on his feet delivering the speech than he can when sitting quietly in an armchair.

Channeled tension can therefore help the speaker. In great part, uncontrolled stage fright is due to improper emotional conditioning. The beginning speaker often thinks of himself as apart from his audience. He is speaking and they are listening. We have stressed throughout this book the idea of a public speech as part of a dialogue, carried on between people engaged in *sharing* ideas. Both the speaker and his audience are thinking about the same topic at the same time: facing the same problems, trying to find new ways of action, evaluating both old and new ways of action. Thus, the speaker is talking *with* his audience. If he accepts this view of public speaking and is well prepared, then the undesirable features of stage fright can be controlled and the helpful and desirable features will remain.

2   Lack of eye contact.

The speaker fails to look at his audience mainly for two reasons: (1) he is confined to his notes because he lacks preparedness; or (2) he is suffering from stage fright. The remedy for the first problem is simply to prepare more fully and learn to use notes efficiently. We shall discuss the use of notes in detail later. The remedy for the second problem can be found in learning to accept the implications of a speech as part of a dialogue. In conversation we normally look at the people we are speaking with because we are sharing an idea, attitude, or opinion with them. We are speaking not at, but *with*, them.

When we look at people, it tells them that we are interested in them, that we are concentrating on them, that we are communicating directly with them. Eye contact is the speaker's most important means of knowing how, or whether, an audience is responding to him. The audience must be a part of the speaking situation. The very idea of communication, of moving another's mind, requires constant sharing of the speaker's ideas with those of the audience. One of the surest signs that the speaker wants to work with the members of his audience on a common problem is his direct eye contact with them.

3   Rapidity.

The beginning speaker is likely to rush through the materials so he can sit down. You may have heard this question before: "Did the man run because he was frightened or was he frightened because he ran?" The point is that, by rushing, the speaker accentuates his own nervousness. When he is speaking too rapidly he has less time to think of what he wants to say, less time to consider his ideas and to perform the physical act of saying them.

The listener also needs time to discriminate between sounds, to listen, to hear and respond, to think about what has been said, to assimilate it, and to work with it. If the listener is not given the time he needs to consider the speaker's point, he may give up trying, and unless his audience is paying attention to what the speaker is saying, he has no reason to be speaking. In short, both the speaker and the audience need time to perform the communication act effectively.

4   Hesitation phenomena.

Most of our speech consists of well-learned sequences of words which make their utterance automatic. As children, most people begin to master the mechanics of speech utterance—the phrases and idioms, the conventionally used and grammatically prescribed sequences of words which soon become habits and roll off our tongues automatically. But at the same time, in near-spontaneous speech, each utterance is a creative act. Any utterance which we say for the first time and which is not an habitual response makes a great demand on our capacity for improvisation.

Speech, at the most elementary level, demands extensive mental effort. Before it takes form in speech, a meaning is something which is not yet defined. Its communication in speech requires that it be conveyed in some kind of order.

We rarely achieve a continuous flow of speech. The speaker and the listener cooperate. Listeners concentrate on the message, integrating elements of it and bridging the gaps which divide the groups of words. The speaker, on the other hand, cooperates by minimizing the gaps in the stream of words and making them coincide with semantic groups such as phrases. Pausing is as much a part of speaking as vocal utterance; it is a basic part of speech production.

Thus, pause has a specific function in public speaking. It permits delay—the time for the thought process to take place. There is no need to substitute ah, er, um, well, now, and the like. The listener will not find a pause unusual. Delay is simply a built-in feature of oral language. Most pauses go unnoticed, so there is no reason to have a continuous flow of sound while speaking. Concentrate on the ideas you are dealing with, gain confidence and a sense of rapport with your audience, and your hesitations will be no longer than the minimal delays which we have come to expect, and in fact need, in spontaneous speech.

5   Lazy articulation.

Many beginning speakers suffer from lazy lips, tongue, and jaw; they fail to pay enough attention to manipulating the various parts of the articulatory mechanism. Most American-English speech sounds are articulated through activity of the lips and part of the tongue. These moving articulators touch fixed or relatively fixed portions of the roof of the mouth or the upper jaw. Quite often the lazy speaker has never become consciously aware of what happens physically when he speaks. Try to feel how these sounds are made: "p" as in pat; "t" as in tin; "c" as in cook; "f" as in fast; "l" as in let. Feel the various parts of the articulatory mechanism move.

However, overarticulation, an overly precise, affected way of speaking, should not be developed, because it calls attention to delivery and hense detracts from the substance of the speech. The best course of action to follow is this: simply do not become lazy about articulating sounds clearly. Make it easy for listeners to listen.

6   Speaking too softly.

Common sense tells us that if we speak too softly, our ideas will be lost. Adequate loudness is one of the essential attributes of an effective speaker. Most problems in this respect are a result of the speaker failing to adjust to the size of room in which he is speaking and to the size of the audience in the room. Practice in speaking under different conditions will give the speaker a good sense of how loudly he must speak in any given situation.

If the speaker makes his audience work just to hear his physical sounds, it may well lose interest in trying to follow the ideas he is expressing. The same thing may happen to the speaker who lets his voice drop at the ends of sentences. Part of his message may be lost, and misunderstanding or lack of attention will surely follow.

7   Lack of vocal variety.

Lack of vocal animation is also quite common among beginning speakers. If the speaker talks in a monotone, he gives no indication that one word, one idea, one point, is more important than others. When a point needs emphasis, a monotone not only fails to help establish degree of importance, but may actually conceal it altogether. The vocally unanimated speaker gives no cues that he is dealing with ideas that are interesting and dynamic.

Most people manage throughout their lives to convey vocal cues to the people they talk with. As we asked earlier, why should the speaker repress animation in the public speaking situation? There is no reason to believe that this problem cannot be cured with a little effort and concentration on the speaker's part.

Once again, the speaker can refer himself to conversation. He can listen to the animation of his own voice—to changes in volume, pitch, inflection, and length of pauses. He can become consciously aware of what he sounds like. A large portion of the problem is lack of awareness.

A student suggested a good technique to develop this awareness. He and his roommate had been practicing their speeches for class with the aid of a tape recorder. Between speeches the recorder continued to run. When the tape was played back, they were surprised to hear the contrast between the animated, dynamic way they spoke in the short conversations between speeches and the flat, unanimated way they delivered the speeches. The student was so enthusiastic about his discovery that we decided to try an experiment with the whole class, with the aid of the tape recorder. As each person stood ready to deliver his speech he was casually engaged in a short stretch of conversation. Then he gave his speech. In the following class session we played the tape back and asked each person to note the biggest difference he observed between the conversations and the speeches. Almost without exception, recognition of the problem proved to be the best way to alleviate it.

Just as a moving object generally attracts more attention than a still one, so an animated voice is a powerful attention-maintainer and an effective cue-provider.

A speaker must learn to use all his resources, among which is his voice. No amount of discovery and practice, however, will really aid a speaker who persistently selects topics for which he has no interest or enthusiasm. An animated voice and animated ideas usually go hand in hand.

8   Lack of body movement.

Just as an animated voice proves to be an attention-getter, so a body that is responsive to what is being said shows the audience what the speaker thinks of his subject, and often demonstrates that he *is* thinking about it. An emphatic gesture underlines, emphasizes, and points to the idea being discussed. Gestures grow naturally from a desire to use all available means to communicate. They should grow out of the subject matter rather than being imposed mechanically from without.

Lack of body movement generally stems from a kind of self-consciousness that the beginning speaker sometimes feels before an audience. When he becomes at ease in his part of the dialogue, his body and voice are free to return to the totality of communication felt in the most stimulating conversations. That includes an animated voice and unconscious gestures.

Check to become aware of precisely what you do when speaking. For example, the speaker who walks up to the speaker's stand and places his hands on either side of it often never gets around to gesturing at all. If the hands are free, there is a much greater chance that the speaker will feel compelled to use them. The speaker who clutches his notes or manuscript also has less chance of gesturing naturally.

Since gestures grow out of the substance of the speech, the relationship between a responsive body and animated, dynamic ideas cannot be overemphasized. Speakers should respond not to a rule which says it is helpful if speakers gesture, but to the reality that communicating an important idea is hard work, and that the speaker must use all available means of persuasion. The responsiveness of the speaker to what he is saying is surely one such means.

9   Incorrect use of notes.

Some notes are generally necessary in extemporaneous speaking to ensure accurate and complete statements of fact and opinion, but they should be used unobtrusively. Improperly used notes detract from the import of the speech. If they become a barrier between the speaker and the audience, encouraging him to speak to his notes rather than to communicate directly, then they will seriously impede efficient communication.

Notes may also facilitate spotty and/or jerky eye contact, and in this way also become a barrier to communication. A common sense rule is to use notes not as a crutch, but as an aid to facilitate the understanding of what you are saying. The speaker who has carefully prepared, who knows what he is talking about, can use them in this advantageous way.

Each speaker should develop his own method of using notes. However, several general suggestions can be made:

1. Make sure the notes are easy to read; otherwise, they are more hindrance than help. Type them if you can; write them legibly in ink if you do not type.
2. Many speakers find it helpful to underline, capitalize, or write in a different color ink the key words and ideas so that they stand out clearly.
3. Most speakers find it more helpful to put their notes on small note cards when they are giving an extemporaneous speech. They are less conspicuous and easier to handle than large sheets of paper.
4. Make sure you include only essential material in your notes. Either a sentence or a topic outline is helpful. Generally, materials quoted verbatim should be included unless they are very short quotes which are easily remembered.
5. When you practice, practice with your notes. Be very familiar with them before you give your speech.

6. Never spend most of your time looking at your notes. You are not speaking to them, but to your audience.

5.3 Delivery

The physical aspects of delivery are shaped by the speaker's purpose, meaning, and all of the work that has gone before: the act of rhetorical invention, the arrangement of materials, the wording of those materials in appropriate language, and becoming thoroughly aware, through memory, of what he wants to say. At the same time, if the delivery is ineffective, the work that has preceded it has little chance of succeeding—for all aspects of the speech act are intimately bound together, and only as they operate efficiently together can the speaker participate in public dialogue with full effectiveness.

If the other steps in the rhetorical act have been handled successfully and the speaker fully understands the *nature* of the communicative act, then there should be few problems with delivery. If there *are* any, first carefully analyze the causes of the problem and then patiently practice to eliminate them and refine your skill in delivery.

When analyzing the causes of the problems, keep firmly in mind how most problems are related to other aspects of the rhetorical process, especially invention. Cicero's conception of delivery, written in the *De Inventione* when he was a young man, is still one of the most useful. By delivery, he meant "the control of the voice and body in a manner suitable to the subject matter and the style."

5.4 Elements of Nonverbal Delivery

1   Dress.

The clothes you wear when speaking can be either casual or somewhat formal. When deciding how to dress, consider the occasion of the speech, your role as a speaker, and your audience's expectations.

Whatever you wear, dress comfortably so that you can move easily. Avoid wearing stiff, tight clothing and noisy, uncomfortable shoes. Likewise, your collar or tie should not be so tight that it restricts your breathing.

Do not wear a hat with a brim when you are speaking because it may make your audience uncomfortable if they cannot make eye contact with you. If you have a tendency to play with your hair, jewelry, or pocket change while you speak, you may want to pin your hair back, remove your jewelry, or empty your pockets.

2   Posture.

The term **posture** has two essential meanings: (1) your body's arrangement when you are standing; and (2) your disposition toward something. It is no wonder then that how you stand while speaking often reflects your attitude toward your speech and audience. To make sure you are sending the right message, always maintain a good posture. A good posture entails standing straight but not rigidly, and squaring your shoulders to your audience, even when you are moving from side to side. Keep your feet at shoulders' width apart and place one foot slightly forward, if you like. Because this is the most comfortable way to stand, it may prevent you from shuffling your feet and locking your knees, which speakers often do when they become uncomfortable.

To stress a point, lean forward or, conversely, convey your dismay or repulsion toward something by leaning backward. However, avoid rocking on your heels as well as swaying from side to side, standing on one foot, and slouching over the podium.

3   Gestures.

Gestures are motions of your body or limbs that, either singularly or combined with speech, express meaning. The basic technique of hand gesturing has three stages: First, begin with your hands either resting on the podium, clasped together, or at your sides; second, initiate the gesture or a series of gestures; and third, return your hands to their original position.

An endless array of gestures can help you convey meaning. For instance, by holding up one, two, or three fingers, you can indicate which main point you are discussing; by bringing your hands together or apart, you can represent unity or disunity; by moving your hand (and arm) to the rhythm of your speech, you can emphasize a point; and by making a fist or opening your hands, you can convey a sense of conflict or conciliation. You can also use gestures to mimic an action or feeling you are discussing, such as the dotted brush stroke of a pointalist painter, or wiping your forehead to convey a sense of relief. However, you do not want to appear overly theatrical by imitating grand movements or overusing this technique. You can represent a sincere conviction or emotion by placing your hand on your chest; or point into the audience when discussing a value they hold or away from them to refer to ideas and sentiments others hold and which the audience oppose.

As with vocal elements of your delivery, you will want to use certain patterns of gesturing to communicate similarities and differences in meaning. For example, create an imaginary grid in the space in front of you, and point to the same place whenever you are referring to the same idea, person, or thing. Then gesture in the opposite direction when referring to an opposing idea.

Finally, try to use an adequate amount of gesturing when speaking, neither too little nor too much—both can be distracting to your audience. Likewise, avoid nervously scratching your face and arms, waving your arms, or putting your hands in your pockets.

4   Movement.

There are three main forms of body movement: (1) You can move to either side of the podium to talk more directly to a part of your audience, (2) you can move to different parts of the room to establish a more intimate connection with your audience, and (3) you can walk toward and away from your visual aid. Unless you are a very experienced and confident speaker, you should never stray too far from your podium. This is especially important when you are using an outline or manuscript.

As with gesturing, use movement to convey the meaning of your speech. For instance, move closer to your audience when trying to build a feeling of trust or camaraderie, and move away from them to signify amazement or disbelief. Never, however, rapidly pace throughout your speech or use movement to burn nervous energy.

5   Facial expressions.

Like gestures, facial expressions convey meaning. As in everyday conversation, use your facial expression to amplify the intent and feeling of your message. For instance, smile at your audience when you begin your presentation, shake your head when you disagree with an opposing argument, give an inquisitive look when something sounds wrong, and smirk when saying something sarcastic. Lower your eyebrows to show sadness, or raise them to express happiness, surprise, or shock. Likewise, lower your head to express sorrow or modesty, and turn slightly to one side, raise your head, and puff out your chest to indicate someone's overwhelming pride or elitism.

6   Eye contact.

Make eye contact with individual audience members and your audience as a whole. Maintaining eye contact with your audience allows you to convey meaning and to read their nonverbal feedback so that you can adjust your speech. Thus, when you see that most of your audience appears confused, spend more time explaining your point.

When seeking to establish eye contact, do not look over the heads of your audience or at their feet. Rather, look into their eyes. Make eye contact both by scanning your whole audience and by looking at individuals in every section of the room. To avoid becoming nervous, concentrate on making eye contact with those individuals who are giving you positive nonverbal feedback.

You should also use your eye contact to accentuate the meaning of your statements. For instance, when explaining something that affects everyone, pan your whole audience. Then, when discussing something that you know is of particular interest to an individual in your audience, make direct eye contact with that person.

Finally, consider the best times to make eye contact with your audience and when you should concentrate on your speech's text. For example, since your initial summary and transitional statements tell your audience something about your presentation's organization, these are good opportunities for eye contact. Realize that you do not have to maintain constant eye contact with your audience. If you become nervous or if you lose your place, pause briefly, breathe, and relax. Then look down at your notes or manuscript and speak directly from your speech's text. After regaining your confidence and the rhythm of the speech, look up from your notes and reestablish eye contact with your audience.

7   Make a conscious effort to control nervous habits.

Listen to yourself speak, and work to eliminate any distracting mannerisms you have, such as rocking on your heels, slouching, crossing your legs, scratching your arms or face, or playing with your hair or jewelry. If you do any of these things, make a conscious effort to stop them, and channel your energy into more meaningful movements and gestures.

8   After practicing your speech several times on your own, deliver it in front of a select audience of friends.

Ask a group of friends to listen to a practice round and make helpful comments. Choose friends who are not particularly knowledgeable about your topic so that they will catch ideas that you may need to clarify or explain in more detail. Friends who know a great deal about your topic will presuppose knowledge of ideas that your audience may not have. They may even suggest eliminating definitions, explanations, or examples that your audience may consider helpful.

When practicing your speech in front of this preliminary audience, present your complete speech without stopping. When you finish, ask your friends to comment on your speech's content and delivery. Ask for comments about your speech's main parts and ideas: For instance, ask whether your main points were clear and well supported, whether your points flowed together logically and smoothly, and whether your introduction was inviting and your conclusion effectively summarized your speech. Then ask about your speech's style and delivery: Ask whether your friends thought particular words and phrases were helpful, if your sentences where too long, whether your delivery was clear and effective, whether you were maintaining enough eye contact, and whether you have any distracting mannerisms or nervous habits. Finally, practice your speech at least one more time, preferably an hour or two before you present it.

5.5 Preparing to Speak

The following procedures may help you prepare yourself to speak during the hours and moments immediately before your presentation. These techniques, along with those that will help you reduce speech anxiety, will help you relax and build your confidence as a speaker.

1 Before speaking, find a place to relax and think about your speech.

At this time, do not try to recall everything that you want to say in your speech. Testing your memory will only increase your level of anxiety. Instead, like the athlete who prepares by visualizing his or her successful shot, pass, or run, use this time to picture yourself giving a successful speech. Think about how you will stress your main points, express your transitions, and make your speech flow smoothly.

2 Prepare your voice by performing a warm-up exercise or two.

For instance, roll consonant sounds like *rrrrrr* or *blblbl* while varying your tone and volume. Do the same by working up and down the musical scale or by lowering your tone for each word in a phrase such as "boo, hoo, hoo" and by raising your tone when repeating another such as "I'm hap, hap, happy!" Using such phrases also provides the opportunity to practice expressing feelings and emotions. To practice your enunciation, quickly repeat a tongue twister such as "Mother makes me make my bed" or a group of similar sounding words such as "slit, shot, slot."

3 Prepare your body with warm-up exercises.

Engaging in warm-up exercises before you speak will make your movements and gesturing feel more comfortable when you are speaking. Loosen your body by moving your shoulders up and down and shaking and rotating your limbs. Similarly, relax your facial muscles by miming big kisses or chewing too many pieces of gum. If you have any nervous habits, such as waving your hands, crossing your legs, or tossing your hair, allow yourself to engage in these actions, and even exaggerate such movements several times before speaking. This will help you expend nervous energy and allow you to concentrate on your speech.

4   Establish a comfortable breathing pattern with a few relaxation exercises.

One breathing exercise you can try is taking short breaths, slowly at first, and then gradually increasing your speed and the amount of air you are breathing. When performing this exercise, keep your mouth slightly open, and breathe from your diaphragm. Another exercise starts with inhaling and filling your diaphragm with air. Next, concentrate on slowly moving the air up through your chest cavity and throat while allowing your chest to expand and your shoulders to move back. Finally, slowly exhale and let your shoulders move forward and your chest and diaphragm deflate. Repeat this exercise a few times. You also can perform this exercise by saying *ah* as you exhale while maintaining a smooth and clear flow of the sound. Because these exercises cause you to breathe from your diaphragm and not from your throat, you should have more oxygen to breathe and, consequently, more energy to speak. These exercises should also help reduce your speech anxiety.

5   When you arrive in the room, walk around to become more familiar with your speaking situation.

Arrive early for your speech, and try to reduce the strangeness of the situation and audience by becoming familiar with both. Acclimate your body to the room's temperature and lighting, acquire a feel for the podium by walking around and adjusting it, and prepare your visual aids. Moreover, make eye contact with some audience members even before you begin speaking. Try to gain a sense of your audience's overall mood, and look for people who use a lot of facial expressions in conversation and who may therefore provide good nonverbal feedback while you speak. If you are nervous, look for audience members who appear pleasant and open-minded and, thus, may react to your speech favorably.

6   Once you are ready to begin, look at your audience to gain their attention.

Acknowledge them by nodding or smiling. Once they recognize that you are about to begin, look down at your notes briefly so that you can adjust your eyesight to reading them, then look up, reestablish eye contact with your audience, and begin your speech.

5.6 Reducing Speech Anxiety

Psychologists, communicologists, and the general public agree that public speaking is one of the biggest fears of most people. Its main symptom—speech anxiety—is an elevated feeling of stress and nervousness that occurs either immediately before or during a speech. A modest amount of nervousness is normal, and to some extent beneficial, because it increases your awareness of the speaking situation. However, extreme speech anxiety can undermine your effectiveness. Regardless of whether your fear is caused by the speaking situation or by elements of your own personality, you can reduce your speech anxiety by following the guidelines and techniques given here.

1   **You will be more confident and have less speech anxiety if you are well prepared and practice your speech a great deal.**

Research and prepare your speech until you are satisfied with its content and composition. Then practice your speech until you can recall your ideas easily while maintaining a smooth delivery. If you have prepared and practiced your speech to the best of your ability, give yourself credit for the work you have done. Acknowledging your own hard work will build your confidence and convince you that your situation is not as bad as you are imagining. Also, realize that many of your audience members will recognize the effort you put into your speech and will sympathize with your fear of speaking. Finally, do not dwell on your past failures as a speaker. Instead, recognize that you will have good and bad speaking days. Know that the more times you speak, the less anxiety you will have, so try to make the most of every opportunity you have to speak in front of an audience.

2   **Have your introduction well prepared so that you begin strongly.**

Getting off to a good start can drastically reduce the amount of speech anxiety you experience throughout the rest of your speech. Therefore, practice your introductory statements often so that they flow smoothly.

3   **When you feel yourself becoming nervous, focus on the ideas in your speech and away from the fact that you are speaking to an audience.**

Speech anxiety may occur if you are concentrating too much on your speaking situation or your irrational fears about speaking in front of an audience rather than the topic that you are speaking about. If anxiety occurs, pause briefly, relax, look down at your notes, and speak directly from your notes. Try to rebuild your confidence by concentrating on your speech, instead of your audience, and work to reestablish your rhythm. Then after regaining your confidence and flow, make eye contact with your audience again.

4   **If your speech anxiety causes you to lose your place or have a mental block, try summarizing your last point to see if your summary helps you recall your next point.**

Speech anxiety may cause you to become so unsettled that you lose your place or forget what to say next. If this problem occurs, try summarizing the point you just made. This summary may help you remember your next point or give you some time to find it on your outline or manuscript.

5   **Breathe comfortably when speaking.**

A major cause and effect of speech anxiety is not having enough air to breathe. When you are nervous, you sometimes forget to breathe properly. A lack of air causes several nervous symptoms: It raises your body temperature, makes your heart beat faster, and restricts your throat. These symptoms not only cause an increase in speech anxiety, but also may cause your voice to tremble, your pitch to rise, and your volume to decrease. Therefore, remember to breathe sufficiently and speak at a slow and steady rate. Pause and take deeper breaths between the major parts of your speech as well as short, full breaths between sentences.

6   **Avoid increasing your rate of delivery when you become nervous.**

Nervousness may make you unconsciously attempt to remove yourself from the speaking situation as quickly as possible. Consequently, you may try to shorten your speech by speaking too quickly or by cutting out a main point. If you speak too quickly, you may mispronounce your words, shorten your pauses, and breathe improperly. To counteract these nervous symptoms, remind yourself that by speaking quickly, you are only making matters worse. Then tell yourself to slow down, pause when necessary, and enunciate clearly.

7   **Limit your use of filler words.**

Sometimes speakers use filler words such as *you know* and *OK* because they want constant confirmation from their audience. If you have this nervous tendency, stop yourself from using such words or phrases, and simply pause instead. You could also use a more formal statement such as "Is everyone following this?" as a way to ask for your audience's approval.

Another nervous habit some speakers have is ending a statement with a vague phrase such as "and things like that" or "you know what I mean." Using such phrases is usually a sign that you are concentrating too much on your audience or that you are unprepared. To avoid this problem, catch yourself before using the phrase, and concentrate on stating your point explicitly. Here again, you may want to avoid making eye contact for a brief moment so that you can express your thoughts more easily.

8   **If being nervous causes such symptoms as sweaty palms or shaky hands or legs, try to relax, breathe slowly and deeply, and move your muscles.**

If these symptoms occur before speaking, take a short walk beforehand, or engage your limbs in movements and rub your hands lightly. To relieve this tension, you even may want to repeat tightening and then relaxing those muscles that shake. When speaking, use gestures to engage your body in slight movements that will keep your blood flowing. You also can relax your throat and shoulders by yawning and rolling your head slowly.

To stop your hands from shaking, place them gently on the podium and try to relax for a moment. Do not grip the podium tightly, for this grip will only cause your hands and limbs to become weaker and shake even more when you release them. Once your shaking is under control, begin gesturing again.

9   **If your mouth and throat become dry, move your jaw back and forth, swallow several times, and keep your mouth closed before speaking.**

Smacking your lips when speaking is often a symptom of trying to create saliva because your mouth is dry. To avoid this problem, drink some water or chew gum before you speak, but remember to remove your gum before speaking. You should also bring water to the podium if you think you will need it. Pausing to take a drink of water is a common and accepted practice that should not disrupt your speech or reduce your credibility. Finally, if being nervous causes you to burp, eat lightly and avoid carbonated beverages on the day of your speech, and then take deep breaths and relax immediately before speaking.

10   **Do not let distractions make you nervous.**

If there is a minor distraction, such as an outside noise or some-one entering the room, simply continue speaking or pause briefly, but do not draw attention to it. If a major disruption breaks the flow of your speech, such as someone yelling in the hallway or your visual aid falling off its easel, acknowledge (or apologize for) it or try to make a humorous remark. Allow for a brief pause to let the incident pass, and then return to your speech. Finally, do not become distracted by a disruptive audience member or one that is giving you negative nonverbal feedback. Focus your attention on the whole audience, and look for audience members who are giving you positive feedback.

5.7 Oral Citations

Because your audience is not privy to your outline or manuscript, the only way they will recognize the sources of your information is through an oral citation. By documenting your research sources with an oral citation, you establish the legitimacy of your evidence and strengthen your credibility as a researcher. To determine how and when to use oral citations, follow these guidelines.

1   Cite those sources that you quote directly, summarize, or paraphrase.

You do not have to cite facts or ideas that everyone knows or that you find in several sources. However, you must provide an oral citation when quoting a text directly or when summarizing or paraphrasing information from a source. Regardless of whether you use an oral citation, you can be accused of **plagiarism** if you copy or simply rephrase a source's language (words or phrases) or style (sentence composition or arrangement of points). Thus, when summarizing or paraphrasing a source, work from your own understanding of the information, and use your own words and compositional style to state the idea. Then use an oral citation to show where the information was obtained.

As in written composition, you will need to cite your source every time you refer to information obtained from the source. Even when you are moving from one point to the next while using the same source you must cite the source each time. Likewise, when first discussing information from one source and then a second, and finally, returning to your first source, you will need to use an oral citation for each instance.

2   Use an oral citation to establish the trustworthiness or timeliness of your source.

As a general rule, you should refer to the source's author, the name of the article and publication, and the date of its publication. However, you may want to cite the publication date only if the timing of the publication is important because it shows that your source was the first to expose a piece of evidence or because it shows that the information was known when someone says that it was not.

3 Be as brief as possible.

When citing a source for the first time, give all the important information. After this, abbreviate your reference with a key word or words by using just the name of the primary author or selected words from the title, and then use this abbreviation throughout the rest of your speech. Do not cite the page numbers of a source unless you are discussing a controversy relating to the text itself, or unless everyone in your audience is very familiar with the text.

Another way to simplify your citation is to eliminate any unnecessary information from your citation. Thus, state only those elements of the reference most relevant to your point and your audience. For example, you can refer to a newspaper article written by a staff writer by citing only its title, date, and name of the newspaper. Likewise, if your source is written by a well-known author and published in a major news periodical, you may want to give only the name of each, because your audience would have no trouble locating the source.

4 Acknowledge your source either before, after, or in the middle of a statement or quotation.

Vary the style of your oral citation to avoid a monotonous speech. For instance, begin one citation by saying, "According to George Will's, November 17, 1998, *Newsweek* editorial. . . ." Begin the next by stating, "'The question is not . . . ,' as syndicated columnist Paul Giguot argues in the November 20th edition of the *Wall Street Journal*, 'but whether. . . .'" Then close your next quotation with a citation such as, "as was stated on the front page of the *New York Times* on November 21,. . . ." When the evidence you are citing is new or uncommon, or it goes against your audience's prior understanding, err on the side of providing your citation before your evidence to enhance the credibility of your evidence.

5 Avoid saying *quote* and *unquote*.

This technique should be used rarely and only for added emphasis. Instead, acknowledge the quotation by changing your voice: pause before the quotation, and then, when quoting the text, change your inflection, volume, and rate as if you are speaking with the author's voice. After stating the quotation, pause again and then return to your original speaking voice.

6 Refer to information gathered from a web site by giving the web site's title.

A web site's title is its official name, and it usually appears at the top bar of the browser's window. If audience members wish, they can find the site using a search engine. For instance, you could say, "According to *Heritage Foundation Online*, ..." However, for a web site that is continually revised, you may want to give more information so that an audience member can find specific web pages more easily. Hence, you might say, "In its August 19, 1998, online article entitled 'Clinton's Troubles Aren't Over Yet,' CNN's *Allpolitics* states. . . .

6

How Words Mean

6.1 The Ignoring of Contexts

In the course of argument, people frequently complain about words meaning different things to different people. Instead of complaining, they should accept it as a matter of course. It would be startling indeed if the word "justice," for example, were to have the same meaning to each of the nine justices of the United States Supreme Court; then we should get nothing but unanimous decisions. It would be even more startling if "justice" meant the same to the robber as to the robbed. If we can get deeply into our consciousness the principle that no word ever has the same meaning twice, we will develop the habit of automatically examining contexts, and this enables us to understand better what others are saying. As it is, however, we are all too likely to have automatic, or signal, reactions to certain words and read into people's remarks meanings that were never intended. Then we waste energy in angrily accusing people of intellectual dishonesty or abuse of words, when their only sin is that they use words in ways unlike our own, as they can hardly help doing, especially if their background has been widely different from ours. There are cases of intellectual dishonesty and of the abuse of words, of course, but they do not always occur in the places where people think they do.

In the study of history of cultures other than our own, contexts take on special importance. To say, "There was no running water or electricity in the house," does not condemn an English house in 1570, but says a great deal against a house in Chicago today. Again, if we wish to understand the Constitution of the United States, it is not enough, as our historians now tell us, merely to look up all the words in the dictionary and to read the interpretations written by Supreme Court justices. We must see the Constitution in its *historical context:* the conditions of life, the current ideas, the fashionable prejudices, and the probable interests of the people who drafted the Constitution. After all, the words "United States of America" stood for quite a different-sized nation and a different culture in 1790 from what they stand for today. When it comes to very big subjects, the range of contexts to be examined— verbal, social, and historical—may become very large indeed.

6.2 Bessie, the Cow

The universe is in a perpetual state of flux. The stars are in constant motion, growing, cooling, exploding. The earth itself is not unchanging; mountains are being worn away, rivers are altering their channels, valleys are deepening. All life is also a process of change, through birth, growth, decay, and death. Even what we used to call "inert matter"— chairs and tables and stones—is not inert, as we now know, for, at the submicroscopic level, they are whirls of electrons and protons. If a table looks today very much as it did yesterday or as it did a hundred years ago, it is not because it has not changed, but because the changes have been too minute for our coarse perceptions.

To modern science, there is no "solid matter." If matter looks "solid" to us, it does so only because its motion is too rapid or too minute to be felt. It is solid only in the sense that a rapidly rotating color chart is "white" or a rapidly spinning top is "standing still." Our senses are extremely limited, so that we constantly have to use instruments such as microscopes, telescopes, speedometers, stethoscopes, and seismographs to detect and record occurrences that our senses are not able to record directly. The way in which we happen to see and feel things is the result of the peculiarities of our nervous system. There are "sights" we cannot see, and, as even children know today with their high-frequency dog whistles, "sounds" that we cannot hear. It is absurd, therefore, to imagine that we ever perceive anything "as it really is."

Inadequate as our senses are, with the help of instruments they tell us a great deal. The discovery of microorganisms with the use of the microscope has given us a measure of control over bacteria; we cannot see, hear, or feel radio waves, but we can create and transform them to useful purpose. Most of our conquest of the external world, in engineering, in chemistry, and in medicine, is due to our use of mechanical contrivances of one kind or another to increase the capacity of our nervous systems. In modern life, our unaided senses are not half enough to get us about in the world. We cannot even obey speed laws or compute our gas and electric bills without mechanical aids to perception.

To return, then, to the relations between words and what they stand for, let us say that there is before us "Bessie," a cow. Bessie is a living organism, constantly changing, constantly ingesting food and air, transforming it, getting rid of it again. Her blood is circulating, her nerves are sending messages. Viewed microscopically, she is a mass of variegated corpuscles, cells, and bacterial organisms; viewed from the point of view of modern physics, she is a perpetual dance of electrons. What she is in her entirety, we can never know; even if we could at any precise moment say what she was, at the next moment she would have changed enough so that our description would no longer be accurate. It is impossible to say completely what Bessie or anything else really *is*. Bessie is no static "object," but a dynamic *process*.

The Bessie that we experience, however, is something else again. We experience only a small fraction of the total Bessie: the lights and shadows of her exterior, her motions, her general configuration, the noises she makes, and the sensations she presents to our sense of touch. *And because of our previous experience, we observe resemblances in her to certain other animals to which, in the past, we have applied the word "cow."*

6.3 The Process of Abstracting

The "object" of our experience, then, is not the "thing in itself," but *an interaction between our nervous systems (with all their imperfections) and something outside them.* Bessie is unique—there is nothing else in the universe exactly like her in all respects. But our nervous systems, automatically *abstracting* or selecting from the Bessie-in-process those features of hers in which she resembles other animals of like shape, functions, and habits, *classify* her as "cow."

When we say, then, that "Bessie is a cow," we are only noting the process-Bessie's resemblances to other "cows" and *ignoring differences*. What is more, we are leaping a huge chasm: from the dynamic process-Bessie, a whirl of electrochemico-neural eventfulness, to a relatively static "idea," "concept," or *word*, "cow". The reader is referred to the diagram entitled "The Abstraction Ladder" on page 85[1]

As the diagram illustrates, the "object" we see is an abstraction of the lowest level, but it is still an abstraction, since it leaves out characteristics of the process that is the real Bessie. The *word* "Bessie"

---

[1]The "Abstraction Ladder" is based on the "Structural Differential," a diagram originated by Alfred Korzybski to explain the process of abstracting. For a further explanation both of the diagram and of the process it illustrates, see his *Science and Sanity: An Introduction to Non-Aristotelian Systems and General Semantics* (1933), especially Chapter 25.

(cow$_1$) is the lowest *verbal* level of abstraction, leaving out further characteristics—the differences between Bessie yesterday and Bessie today, between Bessie today and Bessie tomorrow—and selecting only the similarities. The word "cow" selects only the similarities between Bessie (cow$_1$), Daisy (cow$_2$), Rosie (cow$_3$), and so on, and therefore leaves out still more about Bessie. The word "livestock" selects or abstracts only the features that Bessie has in common with pigs, chickens, goats, and sheep. The term "farm asset" abstracts only the features Bessie has in common with barns, fences, live-stock, furniture, generating plants, and tractors, and is therefore on a very high level of abstraction.

Our concern here with the process of abstracting may seem strange, since the study of language is all too often restricted to matters of pronunciation, spelling, vocabulary, grammar, and such. The methods by which composition and oratory are taught in many school systems seem to be largely responsible for this widespread notion that the way to study words is to concentrate one's attention exclusively on words.

ABSTRACTION LADDER
Start reading from the bottom up

8. "wealth"

8. The word "wealth" is at an extremely high level of abstraction, omitting *almost* all reference to the characteristics of Bessie.

7. "asset"

7. When Bessie is referred to as an "asset," still more of her characteristics are left out.

6. "farm assets"

6. When Bessie is included among "farm assets," reference is made only to what she has in common with all other salable items on the farm.

5. "livestock"

5. When Bessie is referred to as "live-stock," only those characteristics she has in common with pigs, chickens, goats, etc., are referred to.

4. "cow"

4. The word "cow" stands for the characteristics we have abstracted as common to cow$_1$, cow$_2$, cow$_3$ . . . cow$_x$. Characteristics peculiar to specific cows are left out.

3. "Bessie"

3. The word "Bessie" (cow$_1$) is the *name* we give to the object of perception of level 2. The name *is not* the object; it merely *stands for* the object and omits reference to many of the characteristics of the object.

2.

2. The cow we perceive is not the word, but the object of experience, that which our nervous system abstracts (selects) from the totality that constitutes the process-cow. Many of the characteristics of the process-cow are left out.

1. The cow ultimately consists of atoms, electrons, etc., according to present-day scientific inference. Characteristics (represented by circles) are infinite at this level and ever-changing. This is the *process level*.

But as we know from everyday experience, learning language is not simply a matter of learning words; it is a matter of correctly relating our words to the things and happenings for which they stand. We learn the language of baseball by playing or watching the game *and studying what goes on*. It is not enough for children to learn to *say* "cookie" or "dog"; they must be able to use these words in their proper relationship to nonverbal cookies and nonverbal dogs before we can grant that they are learning the language. As Wendell Johnson has said, "The study of language begins properly with a study of what language is about."

Once we begin to concern ourselves with what language is about, we are at once thrown into a consideration of how the human nervous system works. When we call Beau (the Boston terrier), Pedro (the chihuahua), Snuffles (the English bulldog), and Shane (the Irish wolfhound)—creatures that differ greatly in size, shape, appearance, and behavior—by the same name, "dog," our nervous system has obviously gone to work *abstracting* what is common to them all, ignoring for the time being the differences among them.

6.4 Why We Must Abstract

This process of abstracting, of leaving characteristics out, is an indispensable convenience. To illustrate by still another example, suppose that we live in an isolated village of four families, each owning a house. A's house is referred to as *maga;* B's house is *biyo;* C's is *kata,* and D's is *pelel.* This is quite satisfactory for ordinary purposes of communication in the village, unless a discussion arises about building a new house—a spare one, let us say. We cannot refer to the projected house by any one of the four words we have for the existing houses, since each of these has too specific a meaning. We must find a *general* term, at a higher level of abstraction, that means "something that has certain characteristics in common with *maga, biyo, kata,* and *pelel,* and yet is not A's,

B's, C's, or D's. Since this is much too complicated to say each time, an *abbreviation* must be invented. So we choose the noise, *housé*. Out of such needs do our words come—they are a form of shorthand. The invention of a new abstraction is a great step forward, since it *makes discussion possible*—as, in this case, not only the discussion of a fifth house, but of all future houses we may build or see in our travels or dream about.

A producer of educational films once remarked to me that it is impossible to make a shot of "work." You can shoot Joe hoeing potatoes, Susan polishing her car, Bill spraying paint on a barn, but never just "work."

"Work," too, is a shorthand term, standing, at a higher level of abstraction, for a characteristic that a multitude of activities, from dishwashing to navigation to running an advertising agency to governing a nation, have in common. The special meaning that "work" has in physics is also clearly derived from abstracting the common characteristics of many different kinds of work. ("A transference of energy from one body to another, resulting in the motion or displacement of the body acted upon, in the direction of the acting force and against resistance." Funk and Wagnalls, *Standard College Dictionary*.)

The indispensability of this process of abstracting can again be illustrated by what we do when we "calculate." The word "calculate" originates from the Latin word *calculus*, meaning "pebble," and derives its present meaning from such ancient practices as putting a pebble into a box for each sheep as it left the fold, so that one could tell, by checking the sheep returning at night against the pebbles, whether any had been lost. Primitive as this example of calculation is, it will serve to show why mathematics works. Each pebble is, in this example, an abstraction representing the "oneness" of each sheep—its numerical value. And because we are abstracting from extensional events on clearly understood and uniform principles, the numerical facts about the pebbles are also, barring unforeseen circumstances, numerical facts about the sheep. Our x's and y's and other mathematical symbols are abstractions made from numerical abstractions, and are therefore abstractions of still higher level. And they are useful in predicting occurrences and in getting work done because, since they are abstractions properly and uniformly made from starting points in the extensional world, the relations revealed by the symbols will be, again barring unforeseen circumstances, relations existing in the extensional world.

6.5 "Dead-Level Abstracting"

The late professor Wendell Johnson of the University of Iowa, in *People in Quandaries*, discusses a linguistic phenomenon that he calls "dead-level abstracting." Some people, it appears, remain more or less permanently stuck at certain levels of the abstraction ladder, some on the lower levels, some on the very high levels. There are those, for example, who go in for "persistent low-level abstracting":

> Probably all of us know certain people who seem able to talk on and on without ever drawing any very general conclusions. For example, there is the back-fence chatter that is made up of he said and then I said and then she said and I said and then he said, far into the afternoon, ending with, "Well, that's *just* what I told him!" Letters describing vacation trips frequently illustrate this sort of language, detailing places seen, times of arrival and departure, the foods eaten and the prices paid, whether the beds were hard or soft, etc.

A similar inability to get to higher levels of abstraction characterizes certain types of mental patients who suffer, as Johnson says, "a general blocking of the abstracting process." They go on indefinitely, reciting insignificant facts, never able to pull them together to frame a generalization that would give a meaning to the facts.

Other speakers remain stuck at higher levels of abstraction, with little or no contact with lower levels. Such language remains permanently in the clouds. As Johnson says:

> It is characterized especially by vagueness, ambiguity, even utter meaninglessness. Simply by saving various circulars, brochures, free copies of "new thought" magazines, etc. . . . it is possible to accumulate in a short time quite a sizable file of illustrative material. Much more, of course, is to be found on library shelves, on newsstands, and in radio programs. Everyday conversation, classroom lectures, political speeches, commencement addresses, and various kinds of group forums and round-table discussions provide a further abundant source of *words cut loose from their moorings.* [Italics supplied.]

(I once heard of a course in esthetics given at a large midwestern university in which an entire semester was devoted to Art and Beauty and the principles underlying them, and during which the professor, even when asked by students, persistently declined to name specific paintings, symphonies, sculptures, or objects of beauty to which his principles might apply. "We are interested," he would say, "in principles, not in particulars.")

There are psychiatric implications to dead-level abstracting on higher levels, too, because when maps proliferate wildly without any reference to a territory, the result can only be delusion. But whether at higher or lower levels, dead-level abstracting is, as Johnson says, always dull:

> The low-level speaker frustrates you because he leaves you with no directions as to what to do with the basketful of information he has given you. The high-level speaker frustrates you because he simply doesn't tell

you what he is talking about. ... Being thus frustrated, and being further blocked because the rules of courtesy (or of attendance at class lectures) require that one remain quietly seated until the speaker has finished, there is little for one to do but daydream, doodle, or simply fall asleep.

It is obvious, then, that interesting speech and writing, as well as clear thinking and psychological well-being, require the constant interplay of higher-level and lower-level abstractions, and the constant interplay of the verbal levels with the nonverbal ("object") levels. In science, this interplay goes on constantly, hypotheses being checked against observations, predictions against extensional results. (Scientific *writing*, however, as exemplified in technical journals, offers some appalling examples of *almost* dead-level abstracting, which is the reason so much of it is hard to read. Nevertheless, the interplay between verbal and nonverbal experimental levels does continue, or else we would not have science.)

The work of good novelists and poets also represents this constant interplay between higher and lower levels of abstraction. A "significant" novelist or poet is one whose message has a high level of *general* usefulness in providing insight into life, but he gives his generalizations an impact and persuasiveness through an ability to observe and describe actual social situations and states of mind. A memorable literary character, such as Sinclair Lewis's George F. Babbitt, has *descriptive* validity (at a low level of abstraction) as the picture of an individual, as well as a *general* validity as a picture of a "typical" American businessman of his time.

The great political leader is also one in whom there is interplay between higher and lower levels of abstraction. The ward heeler knows politics only at lower levels of abstraction: what promises or what acts will cause what people to vote as desired; his loyalties are not to principles (high-level abstractions) but to persons (for example, political bosses) and immediate advantages (low-level abstractions). The so-called impractical political theorist knows the high-level abstractions ("democracy," "civil rights," "social justice") but is not well enough acquainted with facts at lower levels of abstraction to get elected county registrar of deeds. But the political leaders to whom states and nations remain permanently grateful are those who are able, somehow or other, to achieve simultaneously higher-level aims ("freedom," "national unity," "justice") *and* lower-level aims ("better prices for potato farmers," "higher wages for textile workers," "judicial reform," "soil conservation").

The interesting writer, the informative speaker, the accurate thinker, and the sane individual operate on all levels of the abstraction ladder, moving quickly and gracefully and in orderly fashion from higher to lower, from lower to higher, with minds as lithe and deft and beautiful as monkeys in a tree.

7

Arguing About the Nature of Something

Arguments about the nature of something are arguments based upon definition. Fundamentally, in an argument about the nature of something, one party claims that something is such-and-such, and if the other party disagrees with this claim, the first party has to demonstrate that this something is indeed such-and-such. If the demonstration is not persuasive, the party that made the original claim will fail to win the assent of the other party.

For example, in an argument about abortion, one side will assert that abortion is murder—something (abortion) is such-and-such (murder). Someone who disagrees that abortion is murder will ask for a definition of murder. If the definition of murder that is offered is not acceptable to the disagreeing party, the arguers will continue to seek a definition that the two parties can agree on. Once an acceptable definition of murder is arrived at, then the person who made the original assertion has to show, has to demonstrate, has to prove, that abortion fits this definition.

Sometimes it is easy for the two parties in an argument to arrive at a mutually acceptable definition of some key term. In that case, there is no need for the two parties to argue about the definition. What they may have to argue about is whether the something (e.g., abortion) fits the agreed-on definition of the such-and-such (e.g., murder). And sometimes the two parties cannot arrive at any agreement on this aspect of the argument.

At other times, it may be difficult for the two parties to arrive at a mutually acceptable definition of some key term or to arrive at an acceptable definition of some subsidiary term. For instance, in an argument about whether abortion is murder, the conflict may revolve not around the term *murder* but around some subsidiary term associated with *murder.* The argument may turn on the question of when the fertilized egg in a woman's womb becomes a human being. The two parties might have agreed on the definition of murder as being "the killing of a human being," but the argument might then turn to a consideration of what constitutes a human being. And in our sample argument about abortion, the two parties might focus on the question of when the fetus in the womb becomes a human being. This question can be a very thorny one, and in many of the disputes about abortion, it is a crucial question. The question about how to define a human being is a question about the nature of something: Something (a human being) is a such-and-such (here the predicate term proposes a definition of the subject term, *human being*), as in, "A human being is a rational animal."

7.1 Dictionary Definitions

Definitions are not established in heaven. Definitions are created by communities of people. The definitions that we find in dictionaries are records of the meanings that groups of people have assigned to certain words in their language. For many words in any language, there are several meanings recorded in the dictionary. Some of those are meanings recognized only by people living in a particular region of the country; or meanings recognized only by people on a certain social level (slang words, for instance); or meanings recognized by members of a certain profession (medical terms, for instance). But even those special meanings are definitions established by the consensus of communities of people.

Another fact about language is that words may acquire new meanings or may lose meanings they once had. If the meaning of a word is labeled in the dictionary as being *archaic,* we are being informed that this meaning was once recognized and accepted by groups of people but is no longer recognized or accepted. If a new meaning or an archaic meaning were proposed as the basis for an argument, the two parties in an argument would have to agree to accept those meanings in their discussion.

7.2 Stipulative Definitions

Many arguments turn on definitions that are quoted from dictionaries. Those dictionary definitions will be viable if the parties in the argument agree to accept them. At other times, however, arguments may be based on what is called "stipulative definitions." A stipulative definition is a definition that a particular individual or a particular group has formulated. The definition might be identical with or similar to one or other of the dictionary definitions, but it might be quite different. A stipulative definition represents someone's view of the nature of something.

A stipulative definition will work in an argument if the formulator of the definition can get others to accept the definition—accept it for at least the purposes of the discussion at hand. Another way to put it is to say that a stipulative definition is a "working definition." The parties involved in a discussion or an argument might agree to accept—at least tentatively—a definition of some key term or concept simply to make it possible for the discussion or argument to go forward. Sometimes the parties involved will settle for a stipulative definition because it is more pertinent than dictionary definitions to the context in which the discussion or argument is taking place.

One advantage of the stipulative definition is that it informs everyone involved in the discussion or argument about what a particular key term means in that context. One of the parties says, "Here's what I mean when I use the term _____." There's a certain honesty and straightforwardness about such an explicit designation of meaning.

Some people, on the other hand, adopt a stipulative definition in a particular discussion, but they never reveal explicitly what that definition is. They have their own view of what a key term means, and they presume or expect that others share their view. Deceivers sometimes operate in this fashion. They try to "slip one over" on their audience by using a familiar term but a term that they have invested with a special meaning, which they do not disclose to the audience. In effect, they are seeking to win acceptance by deceptive means. Their deceit will not be exposed unless someone interrupts the discussion to ask, "Wait a minute. What do you mean when you use the term *social justice*?" They may exercise further deceit in answering this question, but if they are pushed hard enough, they may lay out their stipulative definition of *social justice,* and when they do, the audience may say, "We don't buy your definition of the term."

7.3 Examples of Argument by Definition

Let us look at an example of a piece of argumentation that makes use of definition—of an inquiry into the nature of something. One of the topics that was much debated during the Victorian period in England was the relative value of the sciences and the humanities—or, to put it in different terms, the relative value of a utilitarian education and a liberal education. Two of the eminent Victorians who debated this topic were Thomas Henry Huxley and Matthew Arnold. In 1880, Huxley delivered an address entitled "Science and Culture" at the opening of Sir Josiah Mason's Science College in Birmingham, England. Two years later, Matthew Arnold gave the Rede Lecture at Cambridge University, in which he attempted to refute some of the charges that Huxley had made against him in his address. The following is a paragraph from Arnold's lecture "Literature and Science."

1   Matthew Arnold's Definition

Let us, I say, be agreed about the meaning of the terms we are using. I talk of knowing the best which has been thought and uttered in the world; Professor Huxley says this means knowing *literature*. Literature is a large word; it may mean everything written with letters or printed in a book. Euclid's *Elements* and Newton's *Principia* are thus literature. All knowledge that reaches us through books is literature. But by literature, Professor Huxley means *belles lettres*. He means to make me say that knowing the best which has been thought and said by the modern nations is knowing their *belles lettres* and no more. And this is no sufficient equipment, he argues, for a criticism of modern life. But as I do not mean, by knowing ancient Rome, knowing merely more or less of Latin *belles lettres* and taking no account of Rome's military and political and legal and administrative work in the world; and as, by knowing ancient Greece, I understand knowing her as the giver of Greek art and the guide to a free and right use of reason and to scientific method and the founder of mathematics and physics and astronomy and biology— I understand knowing her as all this and not merely knowing certain Greek poems and histories and treatises and speeches—so as to the knowledge of modern nations also.

Here Matthew Arnold is arguing that Thomas Huxley has misinterpreted what he means by the term *literature,* and by doing so, has misinterpreted what he proposes as the proper objective of a liberal education, getting to know "the best which has been thought and said in the world." Huxley maintained that the term *literature* meant, for Arnold, *belles lettres*. The audiences that heard or read both of these discourses would understand what the French phrase *belles lettres* meant. *Belles lettres* comprehended all forms that we mean when we use such terms as *creative writing, imaginative literature, fiction,* and *aesthetic discourse:* poems, plays, novels, short stories, fables, and essays. Arnold insists that in his vocabulary, *literature* is not synonymous with *belles lettres.* He uses the term in its broadest sense, a sense that is recorded in the dictionary, one of the senses that a community of native speakers of the English language agree on: "the entire body of writings of a specific language, period, or people." So when he speaks about Roman literature, he means not only the poetry and the drama of Rome but also the non-fictional, the expository, writing produced in the day-to-day conduct of the government, the military, and the courts.

Are Huxley and Arnold using dictionary definitions or stipulative definitions here? We have made the point that Arnold has used meanings of *literature* and *belles lettres* that could be found in any dictionaries of the English language that existed in the 1880s. In a sense, however, we might say that Huxley *stipulated* what Arnold meant when he used the term *literature.* This stipulation was not entirely unfair. Anyone reading the whole body of Arnold's writings about the "criticism of life" might easily get the impression that whenever Arnold talks about literature, he means "poetry, drama, novels, essays." What Arnold is attempting to do here is correct that impression because if people thought that liberal education was the pursuit only of *belles lettres* or of the humanities, Arnold would, despite his intentions, be transmitting a false message. It was incumbent upon Arnold, who for thirty-five years of his adult life served as Inspector of Schools in England, to correct the impression of his message that Huxley had propagated in his address at Sir Josiah Mason's Science College.

2   James Madison's Definition

Let us look at another example of definition serving as the basis of an argument. The following is an excerpt from James Madison's essay, *The Federalist, No. 10* (1787), in which he defines two key terms: *pure democracy* and *republic:*

> From this view of the subject, it may be concluded that a pure democracy, by which I mean a society consisting of a small number of citizens, who assemble and administer the government in person, can admit of no cure for the mischiefs of faction. . . .
>
> A republic, by which I mean a government in which the scheme of representation takes place, opens a different prospect and promises the cure for which we are seeking. Let us examine the points in which it varies from pure democracy, and we shall comprehend both the nature of the cure and the efficacy which it must derive from the Union.
>
> The two great points of difference between a democracy and a republic are: first, the delegation of the government, in the latter, to a small number of citizens elected by the rest; secondly, the greater number of

citizens and greater sphere of country, over which the latter may be extended.

Once the text of the Constitution of the United States had been approved by the members of the Constitutional Convention in September of 1787, it had to be ratified by the states, securing an affirmative vote of at least 9 of the 13 original colonies. The opponents of the newly drafted Constitution felt that it threatened the autonomy of the states—the familiar doctrine of "states' rights"—by giving too much power to the Chief Executive, to the Congress, and to the federal courts. The so-called "Federalists," who included Alexander Hamilton, James Madison, and John Jay, published a series of 85 articles in various New York newspapers in an attempt to persuade the key state of New York to ratify the Constitution. James Madison, the future fourth president of the United States, was the author of *The Federalist, No. 10,* one of the most eloquent and influential of these political papers.

In the paragraphs of the essay reprinted here, Madison gives his readers a definition of *pure democracy* and *republic.* His definitions of these two terms may have been widely accepted definitions in the last quarter of the eighteenth century, but they have the air of being "stipulative definitions" because Madison prefaces each one of them with the words "by which I mean." Even if the definitions he gives are widely recognized definitions, he wants to make sure that his readers know what *he* means when he uses these key terms. The arguments that he advances in the remainder of the essay for the advantages of a republic over a democracy are based on the "two great points of difference between a democracy and a republic," which he lays out in the third paragraph reproduced here.

Citizens of the United States recognize that the form of government they enjoy, more than two hundred years after this essay was written, is still a republic, not a pure democracy—that is, a form of government in which the citizens elect the president and vice president and the members of the Senate and House of Representatives, who represent them in the making and the executing of the laws and regulations of the confederation of states. The closest thing we have to a pure democracy in the United States is the town councils that still exist in some New England communities.

7.4 Various Ways of Defining

If basing arguments on definitions is an important strategy in argumentation, it would be well for us to be aware of the various ways of defining something—of expressing the nature of something in words.

1   Using Synonyms.

Perhaps the simplest and most common way of defining terms is to give synonyms for the term being defined (the *definiendum,* to use the Latin term for that which is to be defined). Take the familiar word *companion,* for instance. Even without resorting to a dictionary or a thesaurus, most of us could cite at least two or three synonyms for this word: *friend, comrade, associate, colleague, mate, fellow, confidant, confederate, buddy, chum.* Most of us realize that such alternative words are only relatively synonymous. Synonyms may be roughly similar in their denotations but notably dissimilar in their connotations. Of the synonyms above, *associate* is probably closest in denotative meaning to *companion; buddy* and *chum* are probably the most remote in their connotative meaning. The point is that in resorting to synonyms to give our readers or listeners some idea of what some term means, we have to be aware of the degree of interchangeability of the synonyms.

2   Presenting an Image or a Picture.

Another simple way to define something is to present some kind of image of it—a picture, a drawing, a reproduction of the thing itself. Dictionaries often resort to pictures or sketches of artifacts. Sometimes, indeed, "a picture is worth ten thousand words." In the written medium, we have to resort to some kind of graphic representation of the entity we are defining; in the spoken medium, we can display a graphic representation of the entity to be defined, or we can display the thing itself. If we wanted to give a listening audience some idea of what a grandfather clock is, we could display an actual grandfather clock for the audience to see. Television has facilitated the use of pictorial and iconic representations of artifacts for purposes of exposing the nature of things.

3   Referring to the Etymology of a Word.

We can sometimes define a term by giving its etymology—the derivation of the word. For instance, we might give someone a very precise sense of what the word *companion* means by citing its etymology. The word *companion* derives from the Latin *cum,* meaning "with," and *panis,* meaning "bread." Literally, a companion is someone you eat bread with—one of the closest relationships you can have with a person. When we disclose the derivation of a word, we often can give others a precise sense of the meaning of a word. We must remember, however, that words have a tendency to drift far from their root meanings and that therefore words today often have meanings far removed from their original meaning. Our word *villain* derives from the Late Latin word *villanus,* which meant "a farm servant." There is no trace of that meaning in the word *villain* today.

4   Giving an Extended Description or Explanation.

Another way of defining the nature of something is to give an extended description or explanation of it. Dictionaries give succinct definitions of words designating persons, places, things, or concepts. But sometimes we need elaborate expositions of something. For instance, if we wanted to explain the registration process at a university, we might cite a dictionary definition: "the process by which students enroll for classes in a school." But this brief definition might not be very helpful to students registering for the first time at a university. At an orientation session, somebody from the registrar's office might give a very detailed description of the registration process at a particular university—"first, you go here and do this, and then you go there and do that, and so on." In giving discursive expositions of this kind, we might resort to anecdotes, examples, analogies, metaphors, and similes. The medieval *exemplum* was a narrative that was intended to illustrate or support a moral lesson. Teachers of all kinds frequently resort to extended description or explanation in order to elucidate an idea, a concept, or a process.

5   Giving an "Essential Definition".

Maybe the most formal way of defining a term is what is called "an essential definition." This is the kind of definition that dictionaries often give of concrete and abstract nouns.

The formula for this kind of definition is as follows:

Term being defined + *to be* verb + *genus* + *differentiae*

Example: An automobile + is + a vehicle + that has four wheels and is propelled by an internal-combustion engine.

In this example, *automobile* is the thing or the term being defined. The *to be* verb here is *is. Vehicle* is the *genus* or general class into which an automobile can be put. The clause "that has four wheels and is propelled by an internal-combustion engine" designates the *differentiae,* the differences, that distinguish an automobile from other vehicles, such as a bicycle, a motorcycle, a cart, a wagon, or a snowmobile.

An essential definition puts the thing to be defined into a general class and then gives some details that distinguish this thing from other things in the same class. Here, following the *to be* verb, are some typical *genus* terms:

A bridge is a structure . . .
A hamstring is a tendon . . .
A kettle is a metal container . . .

Even abstract nouns can be put into a general class:

Inebriation is a state . . .
A tendency is an inclination . . .
Remorse is a feeling . . .

To distinguish any of these terms from others that could be put into the same class, we have to add some details that differentiate it from others. For example,

A bridge is a structure over a river or highway to provide passageway for vehicles or pedestrians.
A hamstring is a tendon at the back of a human being's knee.
Inebriation is a state of being drunk.
Remorse is a feeling of guilt for one's actions.

The sample definitions that we looked at earlier used this kind of formal definition. James Madison, for instance, defined a pure democracy as "a society consisting of a small number of citizens, who assemble and administer the government in person." We could re-phrase this definition to fit the outlined formula: "A pure democracy is a society in which a small number of citizens assemble and administer their government in person." Frequently, when an argument is based on a definition, the definition of a key term is phrased in this formalistic way.

7.5 Concluding Remarks About Definition

One final point needs to be made about definition as it relates to argumentation: Definition is only a subsidiary part of an argument. What we call an expository discourse could be wholly and exclusively devoted to explaining the nature of something. But in an argumentative discourse, definition serves only as a basis or a preparation for the main argument. In *The Federalist. No. 10,* which we saw earlier in this chapter. James Madison devotes only two or three paragraphs of a 23-paragraph essay to defining a republic and a pure democracy. He needs to make sure that his readers understand the nature of a republic and a pure democracy and the difference between these two forms of government. But once he has laid out his definitions of these two terms, he goes on to execute his main purpose: to argue that a republican form of government is more suitable for the newly constituted United States than a democratic form of government.

As arguers or persuaders, we need to develop a sense of when a definition of something is necessary and an instinct for knowing what the most appropriate form of definition is for our purposes. Most of us have had a lot of experience in explaining or defining things for others, and we have certainly had a great deal of exposure to the explanations of others. Every child goes through the stage of asking such pesky questions as "What's *that,* Daddy?" "What's a circus, Mommy?" Once we got to the stage of being able to decipher the print in a book, we frequently had to dip into the pages of a dictionary to find out the meaning of new words. What this chapter has attempted to do is to acquaint you in a formal way with the function and the process of definition.

C H A P T E R

8

What We Do Argue About

We Argue About Opinions
8.2   *An Argument by Martin Luther King, Jr.*

8.1 We Argue About Opinions

There is another kind of statement that resembles those previously mentioned but that is more arguable than the statements that reflect personal tastes or prejudices: the statement of opinion. Statements of opinion resemble expressions of taste or prejudice in that they represent the views of an individual, but they are unlike expressions of taste or prejudice in that they are arguable. In fact, statements of opinion are what we mainly argue about most of the time. They are the very stuff of argument.

Let us look at some typical statements of opinion:

I believe that the drinking age in our state should be raised to twenty-one.

I feel that the company should adopt a policy of paying an equal wage for equal work, regardless of the sex of the employee.

The winner of the Super Bowl, in my opinion, was not the best team in professional football; the loser of that game was the best team.

All students should be required to take four years of English in high school.

Socialized medicine is the most sensible way for the federal government to handle the health problems of senior citizens.

The first three statements reveal that they are expressions of someone's opinion by using such tags as "I believe," "I feel," and "in my opinion."

But even if you read those statements without those tags, you would see that they resemble the last two expressions of opinion.

One of the skills that readers must acquire is the ability to discriminate statements of fact from statements of opinion. Readers must learn to recognize the difference between a statement like "On Monday, October 19, 1987, the Dow Jones average dropped 508 points on the New York Stock Exchange" and a statement like "The precipitous plunge of the stock market on October 19, 1987 is the price that we Americans had to pay for our profligate way of life." The first statement is a statement of fact. We could verify all the specific details in the sentence by consulting the official records of that event. The second statement is a statement of opinion. The details in the subject part of the second sentence—"The precipitous plunge of the stock market on October 19, 1987"—could also be verified, but the predicate part of the sentence—"is the price that we Americans had to pay for our profligate way of life"—is not subject to verification. This predication represents someone's opinion about the historic event of October 19, 1987. We cannot argue about the first statement; we could argue about the second statement. We might, for instance, want to counter this statement by arguing that the stock-market plunge was *not* a penalty that God or the economy visited on us; or we might want to argue that Americans had not been leading a profligate life prior to the stock-market plunge.

We have now moved closer to the things that human beings can and do argue about. We have seen that, ordinarily, people do not argue about (1) things they can do anything about, (2) events or phenomena that have been established as facts, or (3) matters that represent someone's personal tastes or prejudices. But people do argue about matters of judgment and probability. If someone, for instance, declares among a gathering of friends or relatives, "*Gone with the Wind* is the greatest movie that Hollywood ever made," he or she had better be prepared to defend this statement. If a member of the city council endorses the passage of a new sales tax on the grounds that the increased revenue will spur the economy of the entire community, he or she had better be prepared to persuade the other members of the council that the alleged benefit will indeed happen.

In his treatise dealing with rhetoric, the art that traditionally has been concerned with persuasion, Aristotle points out that the distinctive province of rhetoric is the area of the contingent or the probable—with those matters of human life that present alternative possibilities and with those issues or questions where a plausible case can be made for the alternatives. In a court case dealing with a killing that has taken place, the lawyers do not argue about whether someone has been violently deprived of life (this fact has already been established) but about some aspect of the case that presents alternatives: (1) that what took place was not an act of murder but an act of self-defense; (2) that the person accused of the murder is *not* the person who committed the crime; or (3) that the person who pulled the trigger of the murder weapon was insane at the time.

In essence, we argue about issues where something plausible can be said on both sides of the question. Since human life is filled with contingencies and probabilities there are actually more arguable areas than non-arguable areas. In trying to persuade somebody about something in the arguable area, we have to try to make that person *believe* that the probability we espouse is more likely to happen than other probabilities. In fact, the Greek word that Aristotle used for "rhetorical proofs" was *pisteis,* a noun that derives from the Greek verb *pisteuein,* meaning "to believe."

8.2 An Argument by Martin Luther King, Jr.

Let us look at a segment of a much longer argument and see whether the argument presented in this extract does deal with a matter that is arguable. We will look at a single paragraph from Martin Luther King's "Letter from Birmingham Jail" in which Dr. King attempts to answer the charge that the public demonstrations of his civil-rights groups should be banned because such demonstrations tend to provoke violence.

> In your statement you assert that our actions, even though peaceful, must be condemned because they precipitate violence. But is this a logical assertion? Isn't this like condemning a robbed man because his possession of money precipitated the evil act of robbery? Isn't this like condemning Socrates because his unswerving commitment to truth and his philosophical inquiries precipitated the act by the misguided populace in which they made him drink hemlock? Isn't this like condemning Jesus because his unique God-consciousness and never-ceasing devotion to God's will precipitated the evil act of crucifixion? We must come to see that, as the federal courts have consistently affirmed, it is wrong to urge an individual to cease his efforts to gain his basic constitutional rights because the quest may precipitate violence. Society must protect the robbed and punish the robber.

We will ignore for the moment *how* Dr. King is arguing here, because the method of argumentation is the subject of the next chapter. At this point, we will consider only whether the question or issue is an arguable matter.

The argument posed in this excerpt takes the form of a charge and a refutation of that charge. One kind of issue that is very common in the political and social realms is the *ought* proposition, which often starts out with such phrasing as "We should . . ." or "You should.. . ." The other kind of issue that is very common in the political and social realms is the *is* proposition, which usually assumes the following form: "Abortion is immoral" or "Abortion is not immoral."

The charge here, which was originally made by eight clergymen in April of 1963, is an *ought* proposition: Public demonstrations *should* be banned. The support or the reason offered for this assertion is an *is* proposition: Public demonstrations *are* a cause of violence. (The statement "Public demonstrations precipitate violence" is synonymous with the *is* proposition "Public demonstrations are a cause of violence.")

Both the *ought* proposition ("Public demonstration should be banned") and the *is* proposition ("Public demonstrations are a cause of violence") are arguable. A plausible argument can be made on both sides of the question. The clergymen argue that public demonstrations should be banned; Martin Luther King argues that public demonstrations should *not* be banned. In logic, two proposition that assert and deny the same predication are called "contradictory." Here the proposition that the clergymen argue for and the proposition that King argues for are contradictory. What we know about any contradictory propositions is (1) that both of them cannot be true and (2) that one of them has to be true and the other has to be false. So one party in an argument can argue that its proposition is true or that the proposition of the opposing party is false, for if one proposition can be proved to be true (or false), the opposing proposition is automatically false (or true).

In this case, a plausible argument can be presented for both propositions or assertions. The plausible argument offered by the clergymen in support of their assertion is, essentially, that public demonstrations provoke violence. In responding to the charge and the support of the charge, Martin Luther King presents his own plausible argument. He does not explicitly deny that public demonstrations may precipitate violence (after all, there were many examples in the United States at that time of public demonstrations that resulted in violence). Rather, Dr. King argues that a higher value takes precedence over the possibility or even the probability that public demonstrations will precipitate violence: Human beings cannot be expected to cease their efforts to gain their basic constitutional rights.

Dr. King cleverly compares the clergymen's supporting argument to three analogous situations and expects his audience to give affirmative answers to each of the three rhetorical questions that he asks about those situations. But now we are getting into the *how* of the argument, and the *how* is the subject of the next chapter. The main point we have been making about this segment of a larger discourse is that the parties in this controversy are dealing with typical and arguable issues. We all argue—or should argue—about arguable issues. And at the outset, it is important that we know what is, and what is not, an arguable issue.

9

How Do We Argue?

The basic strategy of arguing is to assert or deny something and then give some reason or evidence to support the assertion or denial. It is true that people who offer good reasons or solid evidence for their assertions or denials do not always succeed in persuading others. But, ultimately, they succeed more often at persuading others than those who rely on loud insistence, the charm of their personality, or bullying tactics. Besides, using the basic strategy is the behavior worthy of creatures endowed with rationality. This procedure is certainly the mark of educated people, and it is the one that will be presented in this book.

Although the basic strategy of arguing is fairly universal, there have been, down through the ages, a number of different ways of executing the basic strategy. These various ways all attempt to accomplish the same end to win acceptance, from one or more people, for the speaker's or writer's view or thesis or proposal or generalization or judgment. But these methods go about achieving this end in distinctive ways.

9.1 Dialogue or Discussion

One of the oldest ways to execute the basic strategy, especially in the oral medium, is a discussion of a particular issue by a group of people face-to-face in the same room. The common term for this way of arguing is *dialogue* or *dialectics*. Students may have encountered this form of arguing in the written medium by reading the *Dialogues of Plato*. In these *Dialogues*, Socrates, a famous Greek philosopher and Plato's mentor, is usually pictured sitting around with a group of students or friends and discussing some grandiose topic, such as justice, the ideal republic, or rhetoric. Socrates usually assumes the role of the leader in the conversation, and his basic procedure is to ask a question of someone in the group. When he elicits an answer to that question, he often comments on the answer and then goes on from there to ask a series of other related questions, the answers to which, Socrates hopes, will lead the group closer to the "truth" about the particular issue being discussed.

Let us take a look at an extract from a Platonic dialogue to see how this method works and perhaps to recognize that we ourselves have engaged in such discussions. We will look at a segment from the *Apology*, the dialogue in which Plato recreates the trial of Socrates. In the presence of the assembled jurors in the Athenian court, Socrates questions Meletus, the man who brought him to court on the charge that Socrates was a doer of evil and a corrupter of young people:

Socrates: And now, Meletus, I adjure you to answer me another question: Which is better, to live among bad citizens or among good ones? Answer, friend, I say; the question is one which may be easily answered. Do not the good do their neighbors good and the bad do then evil?

Meletus: Certainly.

Socrates: And is there anyone who would rather be injured than benefited by those who live with him? Answer, my good friend; the law requires you to answer—does anyone like to be injured?

Meletus: Certainly not.

Socrates: And when you accuse me of corrupting and deteriorating the youth, do you allege that I corrupt them intentionally or unintentionally?

Meletus: Intentionally, I say.

Socrates: But you have just admitted that the good do their neighbors good, and the evil do them evil. Now, is that a truth which your superior wisdom has recognized thus early in life, and am I, at my age, in such darkness and ignorance as not to know that if a man with whom I have to live is corrupted by me, I am very likely to be harmed by him; and yet I corrupt him, and intentionally, too— so you say, although neither I nor any other human being is ever likely to be convinced by you. But either I do not corrupt them, or

I corrupt them unintentionally; and on either view of the case, you lie. If my offense is unintentional, the law has no cognizance of unintentional offenses; you ought to have taken me privately and warned and admonished me; for if I had had instruction, I should have left off doing what I only did unintentionally—beyond doubt I should; but you would have nothing to say to me and refused to teach me. And now you bring me up in this court, which is a place not of instruction but of punishment.

Socrates goes on with his cross-examination of Meletus, but this excerpt is sufficient to remind you of a way of arguing that you are familiar with and that you, yourself, have probably used many times. Here we will not be concerned with the effectiveness or the validity of Socrates' argument but will consider only the method of Socrates' argument.

You are probably most familiar with this question-and-answer method from portrayals of court trials in the movies or in television dramas, or you may have seen transcriptions of the cross-examination of witnesses by the lawyers in actual court trials. One purpose of this question-and-answer method in court trials is to elicit information from the witnesses, but the ultimate purpose of this pursuit of information is to establish a case either for the prosecution or for the defense of the person being tried—that is to say, to *argue* the case in such a way as to convince the jurors that the accused is either guilty or innocent. And remember that in real or fictional court trials, the questioner has a double audience: (1) the person being questioned and (2) the judge and jurors.

Socrates' questions are not haphazard; they are carefully planned. With his questions, Socrates seeks to expose the inconsistencies or the contradictions in Meletus's responses. In the excerpt we are considering, Socrates wants to show the members of the jury just how preposterous is Meletus's charge that Socrates has corrupted the young people who have been his students. So, first of all, Socrates seeks to establish some basic premises: (1) The good do their neighbors good, and the evil do their neighbors evil; (2) People would rather be benefited than injured by those with whom they live; and (3) People do evil things either intentionally or unintentionally. Socrates elicits affirmative responses from Meletus to each of these premises and then uses these affirmative responses to show the jurors how inconsistent Meletus's charge is with the responses he has just given.

Remember that we are not concerned with the legitimacy or the effectiveness of Socrates' method of arguing here; we are just looking at an example of one of the oldest and the most common methods of arguing.

Students are also familiar with the Socratic dialogue through the discussions that many teachers conduct in their classrooms. Instead of lecturing in the classroom many teachers prefer to deliver the "lesson of the day" through a discussion of a particular question or of an assigned reading. The teacher might start out by asking "What is the thesis of the George Orwell essay that you read for today?" Sometimes the teacher will call on the first person to raise a hand, but often the teacher will call on a particular student. If that student cannot state the thesis of the essay, the teacher may try to lead that student to a discovery of the thesis through a series of related questions that the student can answer.

Once the student starts to give responses to the leading questions, the teacher may ask the student to clarify or justify his or her answer. If the dialogue is skillfully conducted, soon other students get into the discussion and challenge the responses that the called-on student gives to the teacher's questions. If the discussion does not devolve into a succession of unsupported opinions and if the responses of the students really clash with one another, a genuine argument ensues. And even those students who did not enter into the discussion learn something and maybe change their minds as a result of the argument that went on in the classroom.

But there is no need to further describe for you such classroom discussions. It is a rare student who has never experienced an argumentative discussion in the classroom. You simply need to be made aware of how common the dialogue form of arguing is.

Perhaps the most common form of the argumentative dialogue is the unstructured discussion of a question or issue that goes on among the members of a family or in a group of friends. Unlike the classroom discussions described above, these informal discussions are rarely planned, and usually there is no leader of the discussion. The argument seems to develop spontaneously and may become very heated.

Let us look at a sample of a typical unstructured dialogue. Let us suppose that a married couple, Julia and Henry, and a dating couple. Mary and James, are sitting around a dining-room table, sipping their coffee at the end of a meal. Julia initiates the following dialogue:

Julia: Did you guys see the movie that everyone is talking about?

Mary: Yeah, we saw it Sunday night. The theater was packed.

Julia: I thought it was the best movie I've seen so far this year. What did you think?

Mary: I just thought it was so-so.

James: Yeah, you know Mary—if it doesn't have a happy ending, she hates it.

Mary: Oh, come on, Jim—you know that's not so. I've liked lots of movies with unhappy endings.

James: Name one.

Henry: What didn't you like about it, Mary?

Mary: Well, I thought the wife was pretty wishy-washy.

Julia: What do you mean—wishy-washy? Seems to me that she showed a lot of backbone when she told her husband that he'd better shape up or she'd leave him.

Mary: But if she had stood up to him in the first place, she wouldn't have had to give him an ultimatum after she discovered that he was having an affair with his secretary.

Henry: How could she have stood up to him in the first place? You saw what an egotist he was. She knew him very well. I guess she was just hoping that after she announced she was pregnant, he would settle down and stop sowing his wild oats.

Julia: That macho idiot settling down? How naive could she get? Or how naive could you get, Henry?

Henry: Oh-oh, she's in a snit again. Every time she starts talking about macho men, she ceases to be rational.

James: I don't agree with you, Mary. I thought the wife was far from being wishy-washy. After all, what could she have done under the circumstances?

Henry: Oh-oh, now the fight starts.

Mary: I long ago learned not to fight with Jim. Once he sets his mind on something, you can't budge him.

Julia: Seems to me, Mary, *you* are the one who is wishy-washy.

Henry: I guess what we'd better do is define *wishy washy.* Otherwise, this discussion isn't going any where.

This is enough eavesdropping on this domestic scene. Everyone who has read this snatch of dialogue has been engaged at one time or another in such a discussion. This informal discussion is a combination of opposing opinions, of challenges about the truth of certain statements, of expressions of personal biases, of jocular thrusts at one another. If this group of friends can agree on a definition of *wishy-washy,* maybe this discussion will go somewhere. Maybe somebody will change his or her mind as a result of this exchange of opinions. On the other hand, maybe all parties in this argument will end up more confirmed than ever in their original judgments about the quality of the movie.

But an argument has gone on here, and this argument is typical of the thousands of such unstructured dialogues that go on every day.

Although this dialogue does not have the carefully plotted sequence of questions and responses that a Socratic dialogue has, the methods of these two kinds of argument are fundamentally the same.

9.2 Induction

Another common form of arguing is the form that logicians call induction. The Latin roots of the word *induction* give us a clue as to how this method of arguing works: *in* = into + *ducere* = to lead—literally, "to lead into." After noting a series of similar phenomena, we draw some conclusion, we make some generalization about all phenomena of that kind. In other words, after observing a number of similar examples of something, we are "led into" a conclusion about all examples of that kind.

When Thomas Henry Huxley was trying to explain the process of induction to a group of working men in the nineteenth century, he used the homey example of hard, green apples. Every time we pick up a hard, green apple and bite into it, we find out that the apple is sour. It doesn't take many experiences of this kind for us to draw the conclusion that *all* hard, green apples are sour. We do not have to taste all the hard, green apples that exist in the world to draw this conclusion; after we have tasted a reasonable number of hard, green apples and have found them to be invariably sour, we could legitimately conclude that *all* hard, green apples are sour.

This method of reasoning is natural and universal. Probably every day of our life we frequently jump to conclusions after observing a limited number of instances of something. This way of reasoning is so natural that, most of the time, we are not even aware that we are reasoning inductively.

In some areas of human life, inductive reasoning is conducted more consciously and more systematically. Polling agencies, for instance, regularly draw conclusions inductively and draw those conclusions according to statistically sound formulas. On the night of a presidential election, polling agencies are able to predict, often very early in the evening, whether a particular state's electoral votes will go to the Republican or to the Democratic candidate, based on the voting pattern in some representative precincts in various sections of a state.

The inductive reasoning of professional scientists is often even more systematic and rigorous than that of polling agencies. Scientists are wary of drawing any conclusion until they have looked at a great number of examples of a particular phenomenon. Generally, the more examples looked at, the more confident a scientist is about the soundness of the conclusion or generalization arrived at. In medical matters, scientists are even more wary about drawing conclusions than they are in other matters. In testing a new vaccine, for instance, medical scientists would want to test the vaccine, first of all, on hundreds or thousands of animals, and then on thousands, maybe tens of thousands, of human subjects before declaring that the vaccine is safe and effective.

Here is a graphic representation of the inductive process:

1,2,3,4,5,6,7,8,9,10, etc. . . . [inductive leap] → conclusion

The Arabic numerals stand for the number of examples of a phenomenon that are looked at; the *etc.* indicates that the number of examples looked at could go on indefinitely. The *inductive leap* bridges the gap between the last example looked at and the conclusion that is drawn. Usually, the shorter the leap is, the sounder is the conclusion drawn. While ordinary people in ordinary affairs are prone to make the inductive leap after considering only a few examples of a phenomenon, professional people, especially in affairs that affect the life, health, or welfare of human beings, are inclined to reduce the extent of the inductive leap by considering hundreds or thousands of examples of the same thing.

A *perfect induction* is an induction that does not involve any inductive leap. If, on a first day of class, the teacher were to ask each student in turn where he or she was born, the teacher could legitimately declare that the data gathered in the survey reveal that 68.7 percent of the students in *that* class were born in the state of Ohio. Assuming that the students all gave a true answer to the teacher's question and that the teacher's mathematical calculation was correct, the conclusion or generalization made from the data would be incontestably sound. The teacher would have made an inductive inference, but the inference would not have involved an inductive leap.

The fallacies that people are liable to commit when they reason or argue inductively should be fairly obvious. For instance, if we make a generalization after considering only a few examples of a phenomenon, we could be guilty of the fallacy commonly labeled a *hasty generalization*. The hasty generalization is so easy to fall into that all of us have probably made hundreds of such generalizations in our lifetime. One cannot say, in the abstract, how many examples of a phenomenon we must consider if we want to avoid the fallacy of a hasty generalization. If the first three times that we ate hamburgers with raw onions we got a violent stomachache but never got a stomachache when we ate hamburgers without raw onions, it would make good sense for us to conclude that we should not eat raw onions anymore. But if three of our friends complained that their 1987 model of a particular automobile had repeatedly been in the garage for ignition problems, we might not be justified in pronouncing publicly that the 1987 model of that automobile was a lemon, because just three instances of a faulty model among the tens of thousands of that model produced every year is not a sufficient number of cases to validate our judgment. The point is that what constitutes an adequate number of examples for us to consider before making a logically sound generalization is relative. In public life and in the sciences, certain conventions about what constitutes an adequate number will guide us in making valid generalizations.

Another inductive fallacy is the result of our drawing conclusions from an *unrepresentative sampling* of a particular phenomenon. If we were doing a survey in a particular city on how the citizens of that city were inclined to vote a month before the election, there are a number of ways in which our sampling of the voters could be unrepresentative: Our sampling could have been done predominantly or exclusively (1) among the members of particular ethnic group; (2) among the members of a particular economic group; (3) among the members of particular religious group; (4) among members of a particular educational level (say, college graduates); (5) among young people between the ages of 21 and 28; (6) among males living in a depressed area of the city, and so on. Not having interviewed a wide enough range of voters would undoubtedly skew any generalization we might make.

In order to get a representative sampling of any phenomenon, statisticians have carefully worked out mathematical formulas for ensuring a randomly selected group. The chances of getting an unrepresentative sampling through random selection are very slight. We cannot guarantee that the generalization we draw from our random sampling will be valid, but the random sampling does reduce the chances that our generalization will be fallacious.

9.3 Analogy

Arguing by analogy is not, strictly speaking, an exclusively inductive form of arguing, but since there are some aspects of this form of arguing that are inductive, we will consider analogy here.

Basically, analogy works by comparison, and in the comparison, analogy concentrates on the similarities between the things being compared. The fundamental principle that governs analogical reasoning could be stated in this fashion: Things similar in some respects can be presumed to be similar in other respects. It is the presumption part of that principle that reveals the affinity of analogy to the inductive process: We can see or we can demonstrate some of the similarities, but we have to make some kind of inductive leap in order to posit our claim that the things are also similar in other respects that we cannot see or demonstrate.

The first point to make about the comparison that figures in analogical reasoning is that the things being compared must be of a different order of being. In this respect, analogy is similar to another form of comparison: the figures of speech known as metaphor and simile. If you compare one man with another man or one city with another city, you are noting the similarities and differences between things that exist in the same order of being—in other words, you are simply *comparing* two things that exist in the same general class. To draw an analogy—or to create a metaphor or a simile—you have to compare things that exist in two distinct realms of being. You can, for instance, compare a human being with an animal and create a metaphor such as "Achilles is a lion in battle"; or you can compare a human faculty with an artifact and create a simile such as "Her mind is like a steel trap"; or you can compare a large metropolis with an ant colony and conduct an argument by analogy.

You may often have heard someone say, "Your analogy doesn't hold." What that person is saying in effect is that your analogy is not convincing because you are overlooking some crucial differences in the functioning of the different orders of beings that you are comparing. For instance, in the just-mentioned argument by analogy between a large metropolis and an ant colony, the person using this analogy may be basing a vital part of the argument on a reference to something that worker ants do invariably because their actions are instinctual. But the audience rejects this argument when it is applied to what the citizens of the large metropolis will do because, despite a number of similarities between the actions of the citizens and the actions of the worker ants in some circumstances, in this instance, the ants will do what they do by pure instinct, whereas human beings are capable of making a choice between alternative actions. This crucial difference weakens, if it does not entirely destroy, the persuasiveness of the analogical argument. In effect, the audience finds your argument to be irrelevant.

What might seem to be a rather obvious caution about arguing by analogy is sometimes overlooked: In comparing something to something else, you must be sure that the audience is familiar with the "something else." If the audience for your analogy is not familiar with the "something else," it will not be able to judge whether what you claim to be similar is indeed similar, and it will be even less capable of discerning whether there are crucial differences between the "something" and the "something else." So do not try to compare the functioning of a municipal government to the functioning of a computer if the audience for your analogy is not familiar with the fundamental principles of a computer.

You should be reminded of what you may often have heard about argument by analogy: An analogy never really proves anything.

Analogies are useful in helping us understand or conceptualize something, especially when something unfamiliar is being compared with something familiar. But as instruments of argument, analogies can only be persuasive, never conclusive.

9.4 Deduction

Another basic way in which the human mind reasons or argues is by deduction. Just as the etymology of the word *induction* reveals the fundamental way in which inductive reasoning operates, so the etymology of the word *deduction* reveals the fundamental way in which deductive reasoning proceeds. An induction leads *into* (the prefix *in*-in the word *induction*) a generalization; a deduction leads *away from* (the prefix *de*-in the word *deduction*) a generalization.

In our earlier discussion of Thomas Henry Huxley's example of the hard, green apples, we saw the way in which induction and deduction proceed. If every time we bite into a hard, green apple we find the taste to be sour, we very soon will be led into making the generalization that *all* hard, green apples are sour, a taste that we do not relish. (If we made this statement in a group of people, someone would be sure to say. "If you think that all hard, green apples are sour, you obviously have never tasted a Granny Smith apple.") So the next time someone offers us a hard, green apple, we refuse it. Our reasoning in this instance follows some pattern such as the following:

All hard, green apples are sour.

The apple you are offering me is a hard, green apple.

Therefore, I know that the apple you are offering me is sour—so I don't want it because I don't like sour apples.

9.5 The Syllogism

The pattern of argument we have just seen is traditionally known as the syllogism. Aristotle is usually credited with being the first to formulate the structure and the principles of this mode of deductive reasoning; the medieval philosophers and pedagogues of the Western world refined, expanded, and systematized the Aristotelian formulation. In the schools of the Western world, students were long required to learn how to construct a valid syllogism and to detect the logical flaws in the syllogistic reasoning of others.

Even in the United States in the early twentieth century, college students were required to take a course in logic taught by members of the philosophy department—a course in which attention to the syllogism was very much a part. After World War II, for the twenty years from 1946 to 1966 when philosophy departments dropped the requirement of a course in logic, college students were usually exposed to a short course in formal logic taught in their freshman English course. Judging by some of the textbooks published in recent years—including this one—courses in argumentative discourse, in which some attention is paid to the principles of formal logic, seem to be making a comeback on college campuses.

It is not absolutely necessary for you to know all the intricacies of syllogistic reasoning in order to argue effectively, but just out of intellectual curiosity, you may want to be introduced to *some* of the intricacies of this form of deductive reasoning. Once introduced to the formulas of this mode of reasoning, you will realize that you and countless other people have reasoned in this way many times without being aware formally of the principles governing erning the structure of the syllogism. If your teacher does not require you to become acquainted with the formalities of the syllogism and if you do not have the intellectual curiosity to find out about those formalities, you can skip the remainder of this section on the syllogism.

Let us start out by looking at the basic structure of the syllogism. The syllogism consists of three proposition and three terms—a triadic structure. A proposition is simply a grammatically simple sentence that asserts or denies something, such as the following: "All human creatures will eventually die"; "Some people in a democratic society can vote in local and national elections"; "Abortion is morally wrong"; "Abortion is not morally wrong" "Cigarette-smoking is dangerous to your health"; "Cigarette-smoking is not dangerous to your health."

In logic classes, it was a common practice to require students to state the proposition in the classic form of a subject term and a predicate term joined by a form of the verb *to be*. For instance, the first two propositions in the preceding list are not stated in this classic form. The first proposition has a subject term (*human creatures*), but there is no noun phrase in this sentence that can serve as the predicate term, and instead of a form of *to be*, there is an intransitive verb (*will die*). Students in logic classes were often exercised in converting such sentences into the classic form. They might convert the proposition "All human creatures will eventually die" into a sentence such as "All human creatures are mortal beings." The latter sentence is now cast in the classic form: a noun phrase as the subject term (*human creatures*) and a noun phrase as the predicate term (*mortal beings*) joined by a form of the *to be* verb (*are*). The second sample proposition, "Some people in a democratic society can vote in local and national elections," could be converted into a sentence such as this: "Some people in a democratic society are citizens who can vote in local and national elections."

The important point to keep in mind is that in converting an assertion or a denial into the classic form, you must not substantially change the meaning. The sentences "All human creatures will eventually die" and "All human creatures are mortal beings" say essentially the same thing. Conversions such as "Some human creatures are mortal beings" and "All human creatures are subject to bodily deterioration" are not equivalent statements, because the second sentence substantially changes the meaning of the original sentence. Bodily deterioration is not the same as mortality (death), and whereas the first sentence says something about only *some* human creatures, the second sentence says something about *all* human creatures.

When people argue, they do not always or even frequently state their assertions or denials in the classic form of a noun phrase on both sides of a *to be* verb. They articulate their argumentative propositions in a way that seems natural to them. But if in testing the validity of a deductive argument, we want to cast the natural-language statements in the mold of a syllogism, we may find it convenient to rephrase the statements in the classic form. The reason for our wanting to convert the statements may be to make sure that we understand the substance and the extent of the arguer's propositions.

Let us look at a full syllogism cast in the kind of natural language that someone might use in an actual argument so that we can see some of the advantages of rephrasing the propositions of the deductive argument in the classic form. The following is the syllogism:

> Those who contribute to the Community Chest can be regarded as being charitable.
>
> John Ogelby has often given money to the Communit Chest.
>
> John Ogelby must be charitable.

In an argument, we might want to ask the person who uttered these statements to clarify a particular proposition or a particular term in one of the propositions. For instance, we might want some clarification of the term *contribute*—contribute money? or time? or services? or what? We might want to know what *charitable* means in this context. Or we might want to know whether the predication in the first premise is made of *everybody* who contributes to the Community Chest or only of *most* contributors or just *some* contributors.

But all of these questions would concern the *meaning* of the propositions, not the *form* of the propositions. To answer some of these questions and to regularize the form of the propositions, we will cast the propositions into the classic form:

All contributors of money to the Community Chest are charitable people.

John Ogelby is a contributor of money to the Community Chest.

Therefore, John Ogelby is a charitable person.

Now, in all three propositions, we have noun phrases on both sides of the *to be* verbs (*are, is*). Moreover, we are in a better position to understand what the propositions are asserting and to apply the rules that test the validity of the syllogism.

But before we test the validity—the logicality, the soundness of the reasoning—in this syllogism, we need to be made acquainted with some further terminology associated with the syllogism. First of all, we must be able to determine the *quantity* and the *quality* of the propositions in the so-called *categorical syllogism,* the kind of syllogism that we are considering here.

9.6 The Enthymeme

Even if you develop an expertise in constructing and testing syllogisms, it is unlikely that you will ever carry on a real-life argument with a series of syllogisms. Although it can be demonstrated that people argue deductively almost every day of their lives, you will rarely, if ever, engage in, or witness, an argument in which the participants exchange a series of confirming or refuting syllogisms. Even Aristotle, the original formulator of the syllogism, would concede that the syllogism is an artificial construction, authentic and useful in its own way but a rather unnatural method of conducting an argument in real life. Have you ever witnessed an argument in which one or more of the participants enunciated two premises and a conclusion? Almost certainly not. But you probably have witnessed or participated in many arguments in which the participants used a truncated form of the syllogism known as the *enthymeme.*

The enthymeme is another concoction of Aristotle's. In his *Rhetoric,* he called the enthymeme a "rhetorical syllogism." In many contemporary logic texts, an enthymeme is the name given to a truncated or simplified syllogism. According to this view, the enthymeme, instead of having two premises and a conclusion, as a syllogism does, has a conclusion and only one premise, the other premise being implied. This notion of an abbreviated syllogism accords with Aristotle's notion that the enthymeme represents the way in which ordinary people reason deductively. Ordinary people do not have the patience or the concentration to follow all the steps of a full deductive argument. For this reason, those engaged in argument with ordinary people resort to a simplified form of deductive reasoning in an enthymeme—a truncated form of the formal syllogism that is more suited to rhetorical situations.

For Aristotle, there was more to the difference between a syllogism and an enthymeme than merely simplification, but there is no need for us to go into a full explanation of Aristotle's views on this matter. We will deal only with the modern notion of an enthymeme—namely, that it is a shortened form of the full syllogism. One advantage of concentrating on the modern notion of the enthymeme is that the shortened form of the syllogism is really the way that people argue when they argue deductively.

Here is an example of how you or someone else might argue in the form of an enthymeme:

Diane must be a happy person because she's smiling all the time.

Here the person uttering this statement is inferring something about the disposition of Diane from the observation that she smiles all the time. The clause "Diane must be a happy person" states the conclusion that the person came to. The dependent clause "because she's smiling all the time" gives one of this person's reasons for coming to this conclusion; another reason for this conclusion is implied and can be deduced from what is said. What is implied is that *anyone who smiles all the time is a happy person.* If we were to reconstruct a full syllogism from this enthymeme, the syllogism would look something like the following:

Anyone who smiles all the time must be a happy person.

Diane is a person who smiles all the time.

Therefore, Diane must be a happy person.

If we were to test this syllogism, we would find that it complies with all six rules for a valid syllogism. Still, many people would not be willing to assent to the conclusion. They would reject the conclusion, not because the reasoning is illogical but because they doubt the truth of one or both of the premises. If they knew Diane, they *might* agree that she smiles all the time, but they would reject as false the general proposition that *anyone who smiles all the time must be a happy person.*

If we were to revise the general proposition to *most people who smile all the time are happy people,* more people would be willing to accept this claim, but in fixing up the truth of the proposition, we would create an invalid syllogism, because now the middle term, *people who smile all the time,* is not distributed at least once. (We shifted from saying *all people who smile all the time* to *most people who smile all the time,* and so the middle term *people who smile all the time* changed from distributed term [*all*] to an undistributed term [*most*].)

Unquestionably, most of us—maybe all of us—utter several enthymemes every day of our lives without being aware that we are reasoning or arguing deductively. Although basically every enthymeme includes a conclusion and a supporting statement for that conclusion, our enthymemes assume several forms. All of the following are examples of enthymemes, but note the variety of forms in which the enthymemes are expressed. In some of them, the nature and the relationship of the propositions are indicated explicitly, but in some of them, we have to figure out which proposition states the conclusion and which one constitutes one of the expressed premises upon which the conclusion is based.

The following are some enthymematic arguments (words that signal the nature and the relationship of the propositions are underlined):

1. She must be from the Boston area, *for* she says "yahd" instead of "yard."
2. *Since* he favors socialized medicine, he must be a Communist or a Socialist.
3. Those Michigan undergraduates are too tanned for this time for this time of year. *So* they must have just come back from Fort Lauderdale.
4. That must be the most popular movie of the year. It grossed 85 million dollars in the first 2 weeks after it was released.
5. The most convincing argument that cigarette-smoking is bad for your health is that a shocking percentage of smokers die from lung cancer.
6. If she drives a BMW, She must be rich.
7. Robert failed three courses this semester. *Thus* he must not have studied very hard this term.
8. Emily is definitely running a temperature. Look at how flushed her face is.
9. Don't tell me that he's a great running back. He gained over a hundred yards in only two games this season.
10. He would not take the crown. *Therefore* 'tis certain he was not ambitious. (Shakespeare. *Julius Caesar*, III, ii, 118)

Words like *so, thus,* and *therefore* signal that the sentence that follows articulates a conclusion or a claim. Words like *since, because,* and *for* signal that the sentence which follows states a reason or the grounds for the conclusion that is articulated. In the absence of signaling words of this sort, we as readers or listeners must be able to figure out which part of the statement constitutes the conclusion and which part constitutes a support for the conclusion.

In an enthymeme such as the preceding argument (8), "Emily is definitely running a temperature. Look at how flushed her face is," we must be skillful enough readers to be able to figure out that the clause "Emily is definitely running a temperature" is the conclusion that the writer is proposing and that the flushed face is the evidence the writer is offering for the conclusion drawn. It would be likewise for any other enthymemes lacking words that explicitly designate how the clauses of the enthymeme are related.

Once we are able to determine what the conclusion is and what the supporting premise is, we can test the enthymeme for its logical soundness. We may have to convert the enthymeme into the full syllogism in order to test it, especially if we are going to run the reconstructed syllogism through the six rules governing valid reasoning. But after a while, we develop a keen sense for detecting the soft spots in an argument. We may detect that the expressed premise is untrue or that the deductive reasoning is invalid. Many times we may find that it is the assumption behind what has been expressed that is the soft spot.

In our BMW example, the assumption that anyone who drives such an expensive automobile must be rich may be the questionable part of the argument. Or maybe we cannot decide whether we agree or disagree with the assumption until we get a definition of what *rich* means in this context. Or maybe we can detect that the middle term in this syllogistic argument was not distributed at least once.

For composing our own arguments and for detecting flaws in the arguments of others, it pays to be aware of the method of argument that takes the form of an enthymeme and to know how to analyze and test such reasoning for validity. We do indeed conduct arguments in enthymemes frequently. We may not necessarily argue logically or effectively simply because we are knowledgeable about this method of argument, but being knowledgeable about this way of argument is not going to weaken our efficacy as arguers either. But such knowledge may make us aware that a particular argument we advance is shamefully shoddy.

9.7 The Toulmin System of Argument

Stephen Toulmin, a twentieth-century British philosopher, proposed an alternative to the system of deductive reasoning that Aristotle gave us in his treatises on the syllogism and the enthymeme and to the system of deductive reasoning that mathematical logicians proposed in the twentieth century. An explication of Toulmin's system of argument is conveniently available in his book *The Uses of Argument,* published by the Cambridge University Press in 1958. Instead of basing his system of practical argument on the model of Aristotelian logic or on the model of mathematical logic. Toulmin chose to base his system on the kind of logic that prevails in jurisprudence, the legal profession. Fundamentally, his system would be concerned with the strength of the case that we present in support of our claims. It is the metaphor of *case* that betrays the affinity of Toulmin's system with the kind of arguments that lawyers present in the courtroom.

Here is a dialogue that conceivably could take place between two friends about an acquaintance of theirs:

"I'll just bet you that Michael O'Malley is a Catholic.

"Why do you say that?"

"Well, I know that he is an Irishman born in Southern Ireland."

"So what?"

"People born in Southern Ireland are almost certain to be Roman Catholics."

"What's your support for that statement?"

"Well, I read in the London *Times* the other day that 93 percent of Irish people born in the southern part of Ireland are Roman Catholics."

"Couldn't Mike O'Malley be one of the 7 percent who aren't Catholic?"

"Yeah, I suppose he could. And even if he was born art Catholic, he might now be a fallen-away Catholic." That's why I said that the Irish born in the south of Ireland are *almost* certain to be Catholics.

Before we examine the reasoning or argument going on in this dialogue, we need to become acquainted with some of Toulmin's terminology—just as we needed to familiarize ourselves with the terminology that Aristotle used in connection with the syllogism and the enthymeme.

The term that Toulmin uses to designate the conclusion of an inference is *claim*. A *datum* is a fact or reason that prompts someone to make a claim. A *warrant* supports or authenticates the datum. The support for the supporting warrant Toulmin calls a *backing*. A *qualifier* is some word or phrase that indicates the force or the extent of the claim. An exception is called a *rebuttal*.

Now we can apply those terms to the various propositions advanced in the dialogue above. (The first speaker makes all the statements that will bear one or other of those terms. The second speaker just asks questions.) The *claim* that the first speaker makes is that Michael O'Malley is probably a Catholic. In response to the second speaker's question, the first speaker cites a *datum*, a fact, that prompts him to make his claim: "O'Malley is an Irishman born in

Southern Ireland." The *warrant* is what gives supporting significance to the fact cited about O'Malley's birthplace: Virtually all the Irish born in the southern part of Ireland are Roman Catholics. This warrant is, in turn, authenticated by the *backing:* a report in a responsible newspaper of some kind of survey that indicated the extraordinarily high percentage of Southern Irish who are Catholics. But there is a *qualifier* and a potential exception (*rebuttal*) to the first speaker's claim: the *qualifier* appears in the phrase that limits the extent of the claim— "almost certain"; the *rebuttal* that would invalidate the first speaker's claim is the possibility that Michael O'Malley may be either a lapsed Catholic or part of that small percentage of Irish born in Southern Ireland who are not Roman Catholic.

Many people find the Toulmin layout of an argument much easier to understand than Aristotle's syllogism. And the statements of the argument strike most people as being expressed in more natural language than the often artificial language of the premises and the conclusion of a reconstructed Aristotelian syllogism. What is missing in the Toulmin system is a set of rules or guidelines for assessing the logicality of the argument. Those who have a firm understanding of the six rules for judging the validity of the reasoning in a syllogism or an enthymeme always have a definite way to go about testing the steps in the argument. Toulmin, on the other hand, seems to suggest that common sense will reveal where an argument were awry. After all, jurors, who are usually not trained in the fine points of the law, are often able to assess the soundness of the arguments presented by the lawyers for the prosecution and the defense in the courtroom. A juror trained in Aristotelian logic might recognize in one lawyer's argument the fallacy of an undistributed middle term, but another juror, although unable to use such labels as "undistributed middle," might be just as confident as the other juror that he or she has detected a so spot in that lawyer's argument.

Thus, many people today feel more comfortable with Toulmin's method of plotting an argument than with Aristotle's method. They feel more comfortable because for them, the Toulmin system seems to be less complicated than the scholastic system of logic, which derive from Aristotle. But the Toulmin system is not as easy a it may appear. Confronted with the text of an argument readers or listeners must still be able to discriminate in the sequence of sentences the *claim* from the *datum* and the *warrant* from the *backing* if they want to analyze and assess the argument. Making these discriminations may not be any easier than picking out conclusions, minor premises, and major premises from a sequence of propositions in a syllogistic type of argument.

10

Evidence and Arguments

10.1 Argument Fallacies

A fallacy is a defective argument that results from a deceptive premise or illogical reasoning. Hence, you should avoid using these arguments and recognize when others do use them.

When attacking a fallacious argument, you should clearly explain its faulty characteristics. In cases where a single argument contains several different fallacies, point out each faulty premise or inference as clearly as possible. Although sometimes it is easy to identify a fallacious argument, other times it is more difficult. For instance, although some people may consider it justified to point out the flaws of a politician's character, others may consider it a fallacious "attack on the person" that avoids dealing with his or her political ideas. Similarly, individuals may disagree as to whether a statement is the legitimate testimony of an authority or a fallacious appeal to authority. If someone might consider that you are presenting an argument fallacy, call attention to the potential criticism and then explain why your argument is valid and not fallacious in this case.

To help you recognize when someone is making an illogical appeal, study the following list of common fallacies:

1   Hasty generalization.

A hasty generalization is an inductive argument that provides little evidence for its claim. The argument's general conclusion usually rests on an inadequate number of instances or cites examples that do not represent the claim being made.

EXAMPLE

After talking with a few classmates, I found that they too were shut out of all the science courses offered for nonscience majors. Hence, the university should offer more courses in geology, biology, chemistry, and physics for the nonscience major.

2 Accident.

An argument by accident is based on a valid principle but one in which the principle is applied incorrectly to a particular example or issue. In some instances, the problem with the argument is that it neglects to consider some overriding factor such as an extenuating circumstance, higher principle, or more important law.

EXAMPLE

In America, we have the right to free speech. Therefore, tabloid newspapers have the right to print anything they want about celebrities and politicians, regardless of its truth.

3 Composition.

Composition is an assertion made about an entire group that is true only about its parts.

EXAMPLE

Every element of the federal budget proposal will help some part or group of people in the country. Because it will help so many people and parts of the country, the new budget proposal is a good piece of legislation.

4 Division.

Division is an assertion made about all the parts of a thing but that is true only about the whole.

EXAMPLE

Because of its rich oil fields, not only is Kuwait a very rich country, but so too are its citizens.

5 Equivocation.

Equivocation is an argument that uses the same term in two different ways so that the inference drawn in the argument is illogical.

EXAMPLE

The Beatles should be considered classical musicians because their songs are classics.

6   After this, therefore because of this (*post hoc, ergo propter hoc*).

This type of argument misconstrues two events that occur sequentially as cause and effect. The argument tries to assert a causal relationship, when in fact, one thing simply happened after the other.

EXAMPLE

Since the Great Society's expansion of the welfare state, there has been an increase in the use of illegal drugs. Consequently, if we eliminate the welfare programs that were created since this time, we will reduce the use of illegal drugs.

7   Weak analogy.

A weak analogy compares two things that have more differences than similarities.

EXAMPLE

Secular humanists argue that creationism should not be taught in the public schools because it is based on religious beliefs and not science. But don't humanists believe in science just like Christians believe in the word of God?

8   Appeal to authority.

An appeal to authority is an argument that uses authoritative testimony fallaciously. The authority's statements also may be biased, misinterpreted, or stated out of context. In some cases, the argument rests only on the authority's name and status and not on any evidence provided by the authority. The argument also can refer to someone who is not an expert in the subject being discussed. In most instances, the authority referred to is merely a popular figure or an expert in another field who is represented as an authority on the issue being addressed. What makes such appeals to authority fallacious as compared to authoritative testimony is that in the latter case, the individual does have expertise on the subject and his or her testimony reflects this expertise. The difference between this fallacy and nominal testimony is that the latter does not represent the individual's testimony as providing direct evidence for an argument, but rather presents only an insightful way to consider the issue.

EXAMPLE

Scientology must be a credible way of understanding the world. After all, many famous people, including Tom Cruise and John Travolta, believe in it.

9 Appeal to the people (*ad populum*).

This argument attempts to justify a claim based solely on its popularity. Such arguments may be irrelevant because the claim should be based on factual information, a universally held principle, an authoritative testimony, or some other type of evidence.

EXAMPLE
A January poll showed that seventy percent of the American people believe that UFOs exist. Therefore, we should recognize that they exist.

10 Appeal to tradition.

An appeal to tradition assumes that value, belief, policy, or course of action should continue because it is part of a tradition. The argument does not give any evidence for why the tradition should be maintained, but claims only that because it is a tradition, it should be continued. Often the tradition being supported conflicts with new social values or new information relating to the subject under consideration.

EXAMPLE
One of the most important reasons why the all-male military schools should not admit women is that they have always excluded women. To allow women into these schools would mean ending a long and glorious tradition.

11 Appeal to ignorance.

An appeal to ignorance claims that because something has never been proven false, it is true; or because something has never been proven true, it is false. Such reasoning is faulty because evidence has not been presented that either affirms or denies the argument's conclusion. Although it is true that the only way to prove something is to show evidence for it, lack of evidence does not prove or disprove anything.

EXAMPLE
Because there is no conclusive evidence showing that the images produced in the crop fields of England were made by either extraterrestrials or forces that we cannot explain scientifically, we must assume that they were created by pranksters and are a hoax.

12 Against the person (*ad hominem*).

An *ad hominem* argument is an attack against an individual's character, past actions, or associations. This fallacy usually acts as a diversionary tactic that attempts to disqualify an argument on the basis of an irrelevant affront on the arguer rather than on the merits of his or her argument.

EXAMPLE

I do not agree with Reverend Al Sharpton's boycott of Burger King and his claim that the fast-food restaurant shows no concern for black communities, because he has made many antiwhite statements in the past.

13   False dichotomy.

A false dichotomy is an argument that presupposes only two positions and recognizes no middle ground or alternative positions. Often, when an opponent cannot refute your argument, he or she will resort to simplifying your argument into a false dichotomy. When you recognize that someone is misrepresenting your argument, carefully restate your position by distinguishing it from his or her characterization of the two extreme positions.

EXAMPLE

All leftists do is criticize the free market. If it were up to them, we would have a centralized economy where the government would run all the businesses and industry in the United States.

14   Slippery slope.

A slippery-slope argument rejects a particular action on the ground that once the action is taken, it will lead inevitably to other, less desirable actions. Such an argument overstates the effects of the initial action and does not consider that other actions can be taken to limit any further negative developments.

EXAMPLE

We should not decriminalize marijuana because if we do, the government will decriminalize all illegal drugs. Before you know it, teenagers will be able to buy cocaine, heroine, and LSD at the local convenience store.

15   Straw man.

A straw-man argument misrepresents a claim, thereby making it easier to refute. This fallacy also occurs by attacking a weaker argument while ignoring a stronger one.

EXAMPLE

According to its proponents, affirmative action is a policy that attempts to provide minorities with equal access to employment, education, and government contracts. Backers of this policy always point to the lack of women and African Americans who hold executive positions in Fortune 500 companies. However, they never want to talk about the lack of white males in the National Basketball Association. By their rationale, we should apply affirmative action to the NBA.

16 Red herring.

A red herring is an argument that introduces an issue that is only tangentially related to the issue under discussion. Often, this fallacy attempts to divert attention from the evidence supporting the claim at hand or simply tries to change the subject.

EXAMPLE

Although most people believe that teachers' salaries should be increased so that school administrators can recruit better teachers, these younger teachers have no idea what it was like for teachers just twenty-five years ago. At that time, teachers had forty students in their classes instead of thirty, and there were no reading specialists or teacher's aides to help students who were slow learners. Moreover, the dress code for teachers was much stricter; all the women had to wear dresses, and all the men had to wear ties.

17 Complex question.

A complex question makes an implicit negative statement about the person answering the question. Answering the question condemns the individual to implicate or accept a negative representation of himself or herself. A classic example of a complex question is, "When will you quit beating your spouse?" To defend yourself against a complex question, point out what the question incorrectly presumes, and then characterize yourself or your position in your own terms.

EXAMPLE

Now, after everything that I said, do you still favor weak environmental regulations that allow you to get rich while the local environment and community get sick?

18 Begging the question.

Begging the question is a circular argument that simply restates one of its premises as the conclusion. The argument provides no evidence that would lead you to infer the conclusion; rather, it simply uses the conclusion as proof for itself.

EXAMPLE

The reason that we know God helped to write the Bible is because it says so in the Bible, and we know the Bible is true because God helped to write it.

Appendices
James Como, Ph.D.

FOUNDATIONAL CONCEPTS

Logos

Liberal Art

Rhetoric *peg K49*

Direct Oral Communcation
your personal "orchestra" performing the extension of natural conversation

Have control of

Verbal
Vocalic - *Rate*
Kinesic

Settings

Private (or Intimate: not a reference to subject-matter) *1 on 1 Convo*
Social *(Party, big group) Not private*
Small Group *(4 or 5 ppl group that's close)*
Public - *talking to the mrml*

Premises
Any connection you have it has meaning to you
Meaning is Connectedness -
We are Meaning Machines
The most important and frequent source of connectedness is another human being. We are "contagious"

Laws

You get what you give ("musically")
In human communication there is always a loss of meaning
Intent never exactly equals impact
Without form there is no fixed or reliable meaning
Without context there is no fixed or reliable meaning

Three D's
what you gonna talk abt.
Discovery — *what you gonna talk abt.*
Design— *put it together how you gonna do*
Delivery - *delivering speech*

RHETORIC

A Summary of the Concept

Rhetoric *The faculty of observing in the <u>particular</u> case the available means of <u>persuasion</u>.*

Commonly the word refers to the *faculty,* and the *art,* and the *skills,* and the *results* of all of these, as well as *tactics* and *strategies* (especially, but not solely, verbal) that account for the effectiveness of those results.

The five *Canons* of Rhetoric

Invention: Discovery—what to say

Disposition: Design—how to organize it

Style: Verbal content—its wording—and other methods of "mediation"

Preparation: Planning and Practice—its mastery

Performance: Delivery—vocalic and kinesic elements achieving presence

The three *Types* of Rhetoric: classically, each was thought to have styles, occasions, and proofs particularly appropriate to it.

Forensic: from the courts, it treats of fact; i.e., the existence of a thing.

Deliberative: from the legislature, it treats of policy, what to do; i.e., action

Epideictic: from public ceremonies, it treats of value; i.e., worth of all kinds

Proofs: that which produces, not truth necessarily, but *belief*

Personal (*ethos*): "source credibility" deriving from the character and reputation of the speaker—intelligence, virtue, and goodwill. Most powerful

Emotional (*pathos*): a readiness to feel, no matter how slight, that can then be directed towards some end. Very powerful

Logical (*logos*): Argument, properly understood!

STRUCTURE

INTRODUCTION: Captures the audience's attention, most effectively by appealing to, or somehow stimulating, the **imagination**. It suggests—but does *not* state—the central idea.

CENTRAL IDEA: A clear sentence—usually a statement, sometimes a question—of the specific topic and its "action"; that is, either what the topic is doing or what is being done to it (the "predicate" of the sentence). When the central idea expresses a *controversy* and thus invites *dispute* it is called a **proposition**, which is *never* a question.

DIVISION: This part of the message functions as a **"roadmap"** or **"billboard,"** telling the audience what is to come. It does so by stating in coherent order the *sub-divisions* of the central idea that are pertinent to the particular function(s) and purpose of the message. Indispensable both to the audience *and* to the communicator.

DEVELOPMENT: Each of the sub-divisions indicated in the division is discussed; that is; each is **amplified** by the inclusion of **supporting detail**, including quotations, statistics, case studies, examples, definitions, explanations, descriptions, anecdotes, and comparisons the **body** of the message.

CONCLUSION: The achievement of a sense of **resolution** or of **closure**. The conclusion may not include a summary, if the message was relatively short and simple; and it may include a hint of "more to come." In any case it does its job best when it makes the audience feel that the *intended* point and purpose have been arrived at. Often, a conclusion is "rounded off" by some reference to the introduction.

Remember that __transitions__ must assist the audience in moving from one section—either large or small—to another. This is especially true of oral messages.

Of course, a communicator may depart from this particular pattern, but only with very good reason—to achieve some desired effect of thought or feeling. And within this structure, as within any, a design based upon recurrent images, ideas, or feelings may be superimposed.

FORM

The *external* elements of FORM—those pressures outside of an "object" (message, statue, painting: almost anything that has an impact upon us)—vary enormously in number and type. In Direct Oral Communication they are such items as time allowed, type of audience, and particular circumstances. Sometimes these elements are very important (as with most speeches), and sometimes not (as with most poems written with the primary purpose of self-expression).

These elements, in combination with *internal* elements, provide "shape" to the object; that is, they invite **expectations**, permit some degree of **recognition**, and allow for **anticipation**. Though a communicator (for example, the author of a murder mystery) may toy with these, finally the object (whatever it is) must achieve two qualities which derive (almost but not entirely) from FORM: **UNITY** and **COHERENCE**. Remember, a human message is an *organism*, a living thing, not a disney-like, animatronic robot. The *internal* elements of FORM are:

1. **Central Idea:** Not merely some vague notion, concept or "topic area," but a well-focused, specific concrete *statement*.
2. **Purpose and Direction:** A *goal* and a clear *route* for getting there.
3. **Tone:** That is, a set of appropriate *attitudes* toward the self, the object, and the audience. These are made manifest (in Direct Oral Communication) by that combination of kinesic, vocalic, and verbal choices often—but misleadingly—called "style."
4. **Structure:** That is, the internal *organization* of parts, especially including *transitions* between them.
5. **Proportion:** A *rhythm* and *pace*, along with the size of—or the time allowed to—various parts, that are "fitting" or appropriate to the combination of all the other elements in the message
6. **Propriety:** Not only good grammar and diction, but appropriateness—that which is fitting and *correct*.

We need FORM. In fact, if it is absent, or even sloppy, we attempt to impose our own idea of FORM onto the object. Needless to say, we are likely to come up with something very different from that intended by the communicator. Maybe something better somehow, but different. Mis-communication (probably serious) will have happened. *Communicating is like making a journey: It's best to know where you are, where you are going, and how you plan to get there, all before you start out!*

Extension of Natural Conversation
Critique Guidelines

General Items

Thinking
What? Why? How?

Designing
Unity and Coherence
Transitions

Performance: Physical, Intellectual, Emotional, Social self
Presence
Vitality
Enthusiasm for the Event
Variety
Concentration, Conviction
Confidence, and Control

Form
Central Idea
Purpose and Direction
Tone
Structure
Proportion

Structure
Introduction
Central Idea
Division
Development
Conclusion

Particular Assignment
Achievement of Specific Purpose
Particular Requirements
Time Limits
Use of Notes

Overall Approach
Preparation: Plan and Practice:
"Conditioning"?
Non-autobiographical
Presence and Reliability of Sources
"Tells it like he lived it"?

Particular Items

Central Idea Specific and clear?

Introduction Attention-getting and relevant? *No initial announcement of topic*

Division Clear, evident and thorough?

Supporting Detail Relevant and natural? Varied? Referenced (as appropriate)?

Vocalic Elements Varied and responsive?

Eye Contact Constant, direct, and full? "Eye shake"?

Subject Suitable to audience and other restrictions?

Tone Poised, varied, and appropriate? Tone of voice? of face? of gesture and of larger body movement? of language?

Rhythm and Pacing Fast enough to be interesting, slow enough to be understandable?

Absence of Noise Strolling? *Vocalized pauses?* Too loud or soft of voice?

Conclusion Achieves resolution ("closure")?

Approach to Audience Withdrawn or evasive? Or welcoming and attentive? ("You get what you give.") "Feel good"?

Logic and Organization Particular subject and approach thoroughly thought out ("Raymond")? Gaps ("communication cracks") anticipated? *Unexamined assumptions?*

Harmony of Sign and Symbol?

VITALITY

Spontaneity and *Immediacy*

Responsiveness/Emphasis/Expressiveness

VARIETY

DIRECTNESS

"Enthusiasm for the Event"

VOCALIC: Pitch, Volume, Rate, Timbre

KINESIC: Eyes, Face, Gestures, Movement, Appearance

VICTION

CON TROL CENTRATION

FIDENCE

PREPARATION *and* PERFORMANCE
Twenty Points

1. The Direct Oral Communicator is always performing

2. That performer is a host: making *conversation*

3. ...and making "music" to go with the words (as with a song)

4. Preparation requires trial-and-error, as well as a gestation period

5. Preparation requires the alternation of planning with practice: but the speech itself—the five-part structure —is always second to focus, research and understanding. You cannot make a speech out of nothing.

6. Prepare one hour for each one minute of speaking.

7. Rehearse out loud, eventually in the presence of others, perhaps using a mirror, audio recorder, or video cam; and time yourself

8. "All preparation is conditioning" (says Muhammed Ali)

9. You don't prepare a speech; you prepare yourself

10. "It's not about me!"

11. "Know the story, put in lifelike details, then tell it like you lived it"

12. Don't act; re-enact

13. There is no such thing as an "audience"

14. "Plan your work and work your plan" (says Sugar Ray Robinson)

15. Magnify

16. If you are a nervous speaker, be counter-intuitive towards your listeners

17. Turn space into place: disturb the air

18. Animate and pervade your speech with your character: sign your work

19. Complying with an artifical setting does not make you a "phoney"

20. Use your entire orchestra: commit!

The Johari Window:

A Picture of the Self

Useful for achieving critical self-awareness

	Perceived By the Self	Closed to the Self
Perceived by Others	*Open*	*Blind*
Closed to Others	*Hidden*	*UnKnown*

Also remember "SPIES". Each of us is:

S ocial,
P hysical,
I ntellectual and Imaginative,
E motional, and
S piritual.

Anyone listening and watching a speaker wants as whole a human being as the speaker can be. *"The most frequent and important source of connectedness for one human being is other human beings."*

SELECTIVE PERCEPTION

We get flows of information through one or more of our five senses: sight, hearing, smell, touch and taste.

Perception can be defined as the processes by which an individual selects, organizes and interprets those flows of information to create a meaningful picture of the world.

Every moment of our lives we are exposed to a tremendous amount of stimuli. Since it is impossible for us to attend to all of these stimuli we screen out most of it out through three perceptual processes:

1. Selective exposure
2. Selective distortion
3. Selective retention

SELECTIVE EXPOSURE In the first process we select what we want to see, hear and read. For instance, we select which books and newspapers we want to read, which television program to watch etc. We, more likely, notice things we need or want to know.

SELECTIVE DISTORTION Even stimuli that we do notice, do not necessarily come across in the intended way. Each person has an organized mind-set and attempts to fit incoming stimuli into pre-existing modes of thinking. We tend to interpret information in such a way that it will support rather than challenge our preconceptions.

SELECTIVE RETENTION We will forget much of what we learn. We usually only retain information that supports our attitudes and beliefs.

Basic Guidelines for Active/and Effective Listening

Guideline	The Bad Listener	The Good Listener
1. Try to discover and retain the interesting part of a story	1. Lets his attention slip away with uninteresting subjects	1. Makes the most of it
2. Concentrate on the contents, not on the way it is presented	2. Lets his attention slip away at "boring" presentations	2. Listens to the contents and does not bother with shortcomings in presentations
3. Keep yourself in check	3. Wants to interrupt right away	3. Does not judge until he/she has heard the whole story
4. Try to discover new points of view	4. Is immediately distracted by details and jumps to conclusions	4. Tries to concentrate on the main idea
5. Be responsive	5. Writes everything down and hardly looks at the speaker	5. Notes down key-words and looks at the speaker
6. Ask questions to clarify if needed	6. Does not show involvement and is inattentive	6. Is involved and projects genuine interest, also non-verbally

INFORMING

A matter of answering . . .
What? or *How?* or *Why?*
(or all of these in combination)
. . . about a single, *Central Idea* stated as a *complete sentence*

1. It is chosen in response to *Curiosity,* which ought to be never-ending.
2. To address this curiosity we undertake *Research,* which includes interviewing, browsing, conversation, and visits to libraries and data-bases, especially the Jamaica library and our York College computer data-bases.
3. We thereby gain *Paideia,* popular, or common, knowledge, that is readily available, even if not handy. Paideia is the *opposite* of *Episteme,* which is expertise, or highly specialized knowledge. We use our Paideia to answer the three questions (What? Why? How?) about our Central Idea.
4. The *Central Idea* must be specific and limited, not abstract, vague or (worst of all) pompous. It should arise from our genuine interests and, above all, our curiosity. It is the *unifying principle* of the entire speech.
5. Our methods for answering the three questions about the Central Idea may include *Definition, Description, Analysis* (breaking down into parts), *Explanation* (showing how the parts work), and *Narration* (telling a story).
6. Our tools in using these methods may include *Analogy, Comparison and Contrast, Definition, Examples, Anecdotes, Statistics,* and *Authority* (usually by way of *Quotations*).

Topic: "movie stars"
   more *specific* Topic—*better*: "male movie stars"
   even *more specific* Topic—*even better*: "Denzel Washington"

A *weak* Central Idea: "Denzel Washington is a movie star."
   A complete sentence . . .
      subject: "Denzel Washington" and verb: "is a movie star"
   . . . that is nearly worthless:
      because it states the obvious.

A *useful* Central Idea: "Denzel Washington is a *complete* movie star."

Sub-points:
   He is appealing both to men and to women
   His movies are generally successful, both financially and critically
   His roles are highly varied: dramatic, comic, romantic, heroic, "everyman"
   He is recognized as an outstanding actor by the public, by critics, and by his peers

---

7. Whatever methods, tools, and specific supporting material we use, *we must cite all our sources!*

INFORMING:
Methods and Tools

METHODS

Definition: the meaning of a concept; its content and associations.

Analysis: the parts of a thing; its "breakdown."

Explanation: how something (for example, a machine, team or institution) works; the way the parts fit together and move.

Description: how something strikes our senses; its look, sound, feel—even its odor and taste; its size, shape, layout, and the like.

Narration: a story; people and events connected in chronological order.

TOOLS

Definition: the meaning of a word; what dictionaries tell us about it.

Comparison: showing how two or more things are generally similar, especially when one little known thing is shown to be similar to something fairly well-known.

Contrast: how two things differ; sharpening the image of a thing by holding it up against something similar in some ways, but very different in others.

Example: an instance, actual or imagined, of some principle, concept, idea or claim.

Anecdote: a very short story that makes a point.

Statistics: *quantitative* expressions; numbers that answer the question, "how much?" Not to be confused with "how good" or "how true" or "how useful" or any other *qualitative* claim.

Authority: support (by quotation or citation) from a relevant expert or a respected figure.

Analogy: showing a similarity or (similarities) between two things that otherwise are completely dissimilar; usually involves mental pictures and other elements of strong imagery.

CONCEPTUAL ANALYSIS

Meaning may be viewed as *connectedness*—connectedness among ideas, images, emotions, things and people. But this connectedness forms in our minds, not in words or in other symbols or signs. Thus, we must work to achieve clarity within these various connections — in our minds—if we are to *apprehend* meaning at all, let alone communicate it to others. By and large, we *discover* meaning, we do not simply "make it up." This is especially important when dealing with language: Yes, in a free country we may say nearly anything we want in almost any way we please. But we are also free to speak nonsense, even to babble incoherently. Legally free, that is. Not intellectually or morally free, because we are responsible to each other and therefore must respect the language which, after all, is a legacy handed down to us and which we must hand down—possibly richer, certainly not poorer—than it was when we inherited it.

These "mental connections," which we must clarify and then convey in language, are **concepts**: *Sets of ideas arranged systematically.* What follows is a procedure for carrying out **CONCEPTUAL ANALYSIS**, which is basically a process of comparison and contrast—of sifting through similarities and differences among various concepts and between very closely related concepts. We are looking for *features*: Those characteristics, or "ingredients," that add up to just this "recipe"; that is, just this *set* and no other. Remember, we are not just defining a word—which is a symptom, or a signpost, or a gateway to a concept—but exploring the intellectual territory that lies behind it. (And remember, too, that a phrase—e.g. "free speech"—can constitute a single concept even though it contains more than that one word.)

1. A **mental survey**: What do I suppose this concept to consist of? Given how I have used it, how I have heard it used, how it has appeared in print, what *might* it mean? Note: I am certainly *wrong*, at least partially, at this early stage. Systematically apply *synonyms* and *antonyms*.

2. Find the **actual and possible** uses, or applications of this concept. At this point I consult reliable and unabridged dictionaries—comparing, contrasting, sifting, along the way. Collect *quotations* that include the concept.

3. Consult **specialized dictionaries and encyclopedias** (e.g. *The Encyclopedia of Social Sciences*) and other reference sources.

4. Investigate the **etymology** of the word(s) or phrase. Examine etymo-logical dictionaries and sources in various *mythologies*, *folklores*, and *theologies*.

5. **Examine with cases**, or examples: model cases, contrary cases, borderline cases, real or imagined cases. *Test.* COMPARE, CONTRAST, SIFT, AND EXTRACT THE *ESSENTIAL* AND *TYPICAL FEATURES*. *Acquire the "recipe."*

SOURCES ON *ETYMOLOGY:*

The Barnhart Dictionary of Etymology	Ref/PE 1580/.B35 1988
Ciardi, *A Browser's Dictionary*	Ref/PE 1571/.S46 1984
Funk, *Word Origins*	Ref/PE 1574/.F8
Hendrickson, *Encyclopedia of Word and Phrase Origins*	Ref/PE 1689/.H47 1987
Shipley, *The Origin of English Words*	Ref/PE 1571/.S46 1984
The Oxford English Dictionary (OED)	Ref/PE 1625/.087 1989

www.bartleby.com

Critical Thinking: 1

Resolving *Controversy* Rationally

Controversy: the existence of *disagreement*, whether major *or* minor, angry *or* mild, loud *or* soft; a *dispute*.... Controversies may be *settled* by chance, violence, coercion, or by *Quarrel*—an unsystematic, unclear, highly subjective, and usually angry clash of *people*.... But all of these are unsuccessful as means for *resolving* controversy.... *Persuasion* (which means "by sweetness") is the most acceptable and effective means for resolving controversy: it relies especially on our *Rationality*.... The key tool of rational persuasion is *Argument*.... Argument is systematic, objective, and open. It allows us to manage controversy by way of *Reasons:* logical clashes of ideas, *not* of people. ... We must work to prevent Argument from becoming Quarrel..., In other words, we must rely upon *Proof,* espcially that *particular type* of proof that emphasizes our *Logos.*

I. Proof: *That which produces belief, but not necessarily truth. There are three types:*

Personal (ethos): "source credibility" deriving from the character and reputation of the speaker—intelligence, virtue, and goodwill. Most powerful.

Emotional (pathos): a readiness to feel, no matter how slight, that can then be directed towards some target. Very powerful.

Logical (logos): Chains of arguments in support of contentions and, ultimately, of a proposition.

II. *Propositions and Contentions (Primary Reasons)*

Statements (not questions!) of *fact* (existence), *value* (worth), or *policy* (action) lay claim to our belief; these *Propositions* are either true, false, or more probably one than the other. In a controversy the proposition clarifies the disagreement by clearly expressing it with a single, short, precise, specific and *complete* sentence. In short, it does not "bridge," it divides.

Propositions require *Contentions.* These are *Primary Reasons* for the proposition. They must be argued (supported with logical arguments) before we *rationally* can choose one side or the other of a proposition.

There are never more than a handful of contentions in a proposition (either for or against it). However, we must be careful: some statements are very appealing, even true, and are *in*directly related to the proposition: they *seem* like contentions. but they are not. *The connection between the contention and the proposition must always be direct and indispensable.*

III. *Arguments (Secondary Reasons)*

Arguments are the reasons for our Contentions; "Secondary Reasons" that support the Primary Reasons. To make them we *match* something in the world ("evidence") to something in our minds ("warrant"—some *conception* which ought to be as clear, as systematic, and as sound as we can make it), and then we infer a claim, even if that claim is only partial ("qualified").

The parts of an argument are Evidence, Backing (for the Evidence: "Who says, how, and why?"), Claim (the inference), Warrant (which joins the Evidence and the Claim), Backing (for the Warrant), and Reservations (possible exceptions, the number and force of which determine the degree of qualification). A quick device for checking an argument is to link these parts by (in order) the common words "therefore," "since," "after all" (to link Backings) and "unless."

Some Points About
SPEECH THREE

Your job is to convince: that is, to bring your listeners closer to agreement with you than they were before you spoke.... Your proposition should be of interest to you, of course, but also practical; it might be humorous or even a bit ridiculous.... The time limits are 5–8 minutes; notes are allowed on 3″ × 5″ index cards, with the number of cards indicated by your instructor.

TASKS
Proposition
Background (historical and social context)
Key concepts (definitions)
Contentions (primary reasons)
Arguments (secondary reasons)

PROPOSITION (sample)
Capital punishment should be abolished.

CONTENTIONS (sample)
1. It is immoral to take a helpless human life.
2. It generally fails to deter serious crime.
3. It is catastrophically irreversible in the event of error.
4. Retribution can be achieved by other means even for the most heinous crimes.
5. It is (still) inequitably applied to the poor and to people of color and will likely remain so for the foreseeable future.

Genuine or Fake Contentions?
6. It is generally more costly than life imprisonment.
7. As "cruel and unusual punishment," it violates the United States Constitution.

DIVISION (sample)
Background
Will describe the three stages of capital punishment in U.S. history, including two Supreme Court decisions and a comparison to the rest of the world.

Contentions (see above)
Nos. 1–5 (of course, these must be completely stated).

Selected Contentions (contentions selected for actual argument in the speech)

Will argue nos. 1, 2, 4 (these must be completely stated).

Key Concepts (these may be defined together in one place or as they arise in the speech)

Will define *Immoral, Deter, Retribution* (taken from contentions 1, 2, & 4).

Evidence for ARGUMENT for Contention no. 2 (sample)

1. Six states that have eliminated C.P. have had a *decline* in serous crime
2. Seven states that have brought back or increased the frequency of C.P. have seen a *rise* in serious crime.
3. 87% of prisoners on Death Row who responded to a poll said that, knowing what they know now, being where they are now, and facing what they are facing now—they *would* commit the same crime again.

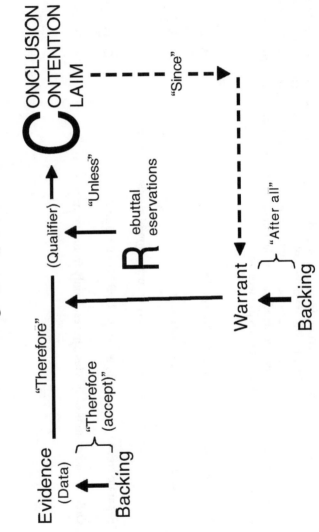

An Argument:
According to Stephen Toulmin

Crocodiles are very old types of animal life. Their fossils are found in all geological strata. Now, newer fossil crocodiles are more like our modern species, while older fossils are quite unlike. In other words, there is an orderly succession of slightly differing species leading from remote times to the present day. Of course, this orderly succession could be explained by saying that God created the many species and arranged them in just this order. But obviously the proper explanation is Evolution: that each species gradually evolved from its predecessor.

1. _____ New fossils are more like our modern species; older fossils more unlike.

2. _____ Crocodiles are a very old type of animal life.

3. _____ The theory of Evolution best explains the succession of species of crocodiles.

4. _____ Separate creation and arrangement by God is unthinkable.

5. _____ Orderly successions of species can result only from Evolution.

A. Irrelevant

B. Backing

C. Conclusion

D. Warrant

E. Evidence

You hold that the Constitution protects slavery in the territories, and you have sworn to support that Constitution. Surely, then, it is utterly inconsistent for you to say that local territorial communities may pass laws against slavery. "Support the Constitution" always means opposing laws that are contrary to the Constitution. If it does not mean that, it has no meaning at all. —from A. Lincoln, Lincoln-Douglas debates, 1858.

____1. It is inconsistent for you to say that local communities may pass laws against slavery.

____2. "Support the Constitution" always means opposing laws contrary to the Constitution.

____3. You should not violate and disregard your oath.

____4. You hold that the Constitution protects slavery in the territories, and have sworn to support that Constitution.

____5. "Support that Constitution" means nothing if it does not mean opposing laws contrary to the Constitution.

A. None of these

B. Backing for Warrant

C. Conclusion

D. Warrant

E. Evidence

Gentlemen, I want you to suppose a case for a moment. Suppose that all the property you were worth was in gold, and you had put it in the hands of Blondin, the famous rope-walker, to carry across Niagara Falls on a tight-rope. Would you shake the rope while he was walking over it, or keep shouting to him, "Blondin, stoop a little more! Go a little faster!"? No, I'm sure you would not. Now, your government is in the same situation. It is carrying immense weight over a stormy ocean. Untold treasure are in its hands. It is doing the best it can. Don't badger it. Just keep still, and it will get you safely across. — Abraham Lincoln, in reply to Northern critics who thought the civil war was moving too slowly.

____1 Experience of many common situations, like climbing, driving, etc. shows that competent people are more likely to succeed when not distracted by advice in the pinch.

A. Irrelevant

____2 Blondin would be more likely to succeed if onlookers did not badger him.

B. Backing

____3 The safety of the nation is more valuable than all of your property.

C. Conclusion

____4 The government will get you through the war safely if you do not give it a lot of criticism.

D. Warrant

____5 Competent people in dangerous situations, like rope-walking and fighting wars, operate better when they are not given advice at the critical moment.

E. Evidence

Key Terms

Argument. Evidence (outside the mind) *matched* to a warrant (inside the mind, a concept) leading to a conclusion.

Argumentation. The discovery and formulation of the logical requirements for proof of a given proposition.

Central Idea. The "spine" of a message; its focus. Usually a single statement, though sometimes a specific question. Everything in the message has to be connected to it.

Coherence. The quality of a message that results when each piece is in its correct place so that all the pieces add up to single picture.

Concept. A set of ideas arranged systematically. Concepts exist only in the mind.

Conceptual Thinking. A process whereby features of a concept are *abstracted* from various sources (e.g. etymologies, examples) then sifted, compared and contrasted in order to discern those that are either essential to, or typical of, a given concept.

Contention. Primary reasons (expressed as statements) for a proposition. Usually numbering no more than four or five, they are answer to issues.

Counter-intuitive. The opposite of a "hunch" or a "feeling" or even of "common sense, it is thinking that goes against the grain and, if correct, usually has solid (though not obvious) logic behind it, as when a driving teacher tells a person learning how to drive to "steer *into* the skid."

Critical Thinking. Thinking that is 1/ reasonable, 2/ conducive to judgment that relies on objective criteria, 3/ sensitive to context, and 4/ self-corrective.

D's: Discovery, Design, Delivery.

Discovery. (Also known as *Invention* [from Latin `invenire'—"to find"]). The first of the five canons (or parts) of Rhetoric, it *discovers* (finds) what so say, from the formulation of propositions, to the discovery of contentions, to supporting matter for the contentions, and on to the formulation of proofs, especially logical arguments. It consumes nearly the whole of Aristotle's *Rhetoric* and is the origin of the discipline of Critical Thinking.

Entropy. A concept borrowed from physics, it is (very briefly) the tendency of things to fall apart, and it is everywhere, especially in human communication.

Extemporaneous. Not to be confused with impromptu or improvisation, it is a thought-out and practiced mode of speaking that is *not* written down, read, or recited from memory; it is how we converse most of the time.

Extension of Natural Conversation. Extemporaneous public communication.

Fallacy. Any error, abuse, or neglect of reasoning.

Form. The shape of a message, including its purpose, direction, and structure; the expectations it invites; and the reliable anticipation that it stirs in a reader or listener. Form is marked by restraint, outside elements (e.g. time limits) and inside elements (e.g. a central idea) that keep it integrated.

Issue. A closed-ended *constitutive* question about a proposition. A point of *stasis* ("strife"). The answer to an issue is a *contention.*

Johari Window. A model of an individual self as a window with four panes: an open self, a hidden self, a blind self, and an unknown self. It is in the interest of a performer (i.e. a public communicator) to attempt a whole view of his or her self—that is, to be critically self—aware—so that his or her "orchestra" plays the music actually intended.

Kinesic. Any and all movement of the performer, from shifty eyes to wild pacing; what the audience sees.

Liberal Art. A body of knowledge (e.g. rhetoric, history, chemistry) designed to "set us free," both from a slavish dependence upon the things of the world and from ignorance. It helps us to fill our spare time (i.e., time after we've "filled our bellies") and thus to maximize our humanity.

"Music." If speech is like a song, with both words and music, then the music of speech is everything that accompanies the actual language, from tone of voice to tone of dress and tone of face—and so on. It is the atmosphere or feel or vibe that will "infect" the audience.

"Noise." Not just sound, it is *anything* that disrupts or *tends to disrupt* communication. It is all around us and inescapable; though it can be minimized it cannot be eliminated.

Oral. By mouth. Any sound—from words to growls to laughter—is oral communication. If the sound is a spoken word then it is *both* oral *and* verbal.

"Orchestra." The collection of instruments (voice, face, dress, mood, *Logos*) that each speaker possesses and should use to communicate. Of course, each instrument should be playing its part of the same music (mixed messages, like discordant music, confuses people and sometimes makes them both frightened and angry); and so the orchestra needs its conductor, that well-prepared mind that has chosen the music and that knows the orchestra.

148

Performer. Any and all direct oral communicator, from the mutterer to the accomplished orator. One may not know, like, or care about performing, but it cannot be avoided, since the speaker *is*, more or less, the speech. As the poet W.B. Yeats wrote, we "cannot separate the dancer from the dance."

Presence. Often (even if mistakenly) called charisma, it is a combination of poise, self-possession, and sense of belonging that allows a performer "to turn space into place."

Proposition. A declarative sentence of fact (existence), of value (worth), or of policy (action) expressing a judgment.

Redundancy. Reinforcement, as when on a personal check we write the amount in both numbers and words. In speaking it can be anything from an internal summary, to repetition, to vocal inflection, dress, or movements that back up the words, as when we twist our faces and shout, "I am angry!"

Rhetoric. The *faculty* of discovering in the particular case the available means of *persuasion.*

Selective Perception. Our tendency to expose ourselves to messages we prefer (thus screening out others), to pay attention only to a small portion of those messages, and then to remember an even smaller portion of what we paid attention to; in other words, we come away from an event or a subject with only a very small portion of the whole.

Sign. A sound (like a grunt), movement (like pointing) or an object like a green arrow on the bottom circle of a traffic light that points to something close by in time and space or that directs behavior "here and now."

Solipsism. From the two Latin words *solo* ("alone") and *ipse* ("self"), this way of thinking dictates that value (for example, moral value), meaning, and most judgments are subjective; that is, they are whatever any given (*solo*) person (*ipse*) says, or, more accurately, "feels."

Structure. The intended and useful assembly of a message, a basic one being the classical five-part structure of Introduction, Central Idea, Division, Development, Conclusion.

Symbol. Anything (for example, all words) that points to something in the mind (e.g. a concept) rather than actually in the world (which is the function of a sign).

Toulmin Model. The conception of an argument devised by the philosopher Stephen Toulmin. It consists of various parts (e.g. Evidence or Data, Warrant, Conclusion) connected by ordinary language (e.g. "therefore," "since," "unless") and (unlike its original source, the Syllogism) mimics the way people actually think of and speak their reasons for a belief. A very convenient (and relatively easily-learned) method for constructing, and assessing the validity of, reasons in ordinary, everyday exchanges, in public communication (such as political speaking), and in hard critical thinking generally.

Unity. The quality of a message that results when all the elements of a message belong in the message (that is, are somehow connected to the central idea) and when no important element is missing.

Verbal. Communication by words, in any way, shape or form—including written, signed (in some sign languages) or as Morse code in an old-fashioned telegram. Not to be confused with spoken communication which, if including words, is *both* oral *and* verbal: the verbal element is the word itself, the oral element is its vocalic accompaniment.

Vocalic. The utterance of sound: that combination of pitch, rate, volume and timbre yield what we properly call vocal intonation, or tone-of-voice.